Byron

Paul Fearne

chipmunkapublishing
the mental health publisher

All rights reserved, no part of this publication may be reproduced by any means, electronic, mechanical photocopying, documentary, film or in any other format without prior written permission of the publisher.

> Published by
> Chipmunkapublishing
> United Kingdom

http://www.chipmunkapublishing.com

Copyright © Paul Fearne 2022

ISBN   978-1-78382-6346

Paul Fearne

This is a book addressed to the 19th century English poet, Lord Byron. Byron underwent many adventures, from going into exile from England, to his death fighting for Greek independence.

This is a work of prose poetry, and should be read in this mode. There is no greater accolade for Byron, I believe, that to write a work addressed to him in poetic prose – poetry being his chief form of expression.

Byron

Paul Fearne

Byron – Let us settle into the night. Let us be the ones never to shudder. Come and be my guide on this grand journey. I am the one to see things as clearly as the day, but what I have got, but the sandal to the shoe. Have nothing to fear.

Do not be shy, listen carefully, there is no time to be dismayed. There are things that we laugh for, and things that we have no need of. And then, with the deepest vein to beggar a bond, there will be a slight intransigence of the morrow. Be kind.

Byron – Your first translations from the Greek, at Harrow. From Aeschylus, and from there your love grew. Finally to Greece to help them break the yoke. And then, gushing into it, like the mire in times of need. Come forth, you are tallied.

From utmost feeling, no matter how deep. No matter how elongated. There is a time that has no passing cloud, no time to rest. Be the fruit on the vines, and yours will be a sequence of events that changes a world. Do that, and freedom will be yours.

Byron - Lost to the nemesis, your life adheres to every point. And then the laughing, the laughing at our expense. There can be no more of the troop, as the windswept ego lavishes praise on the unwary. What is there to do, but blow a gale.

Longing, and a sense of calm. I write as I see it, and yours is a life worth might. Do not unbind the swing, there are things we must do. And here, where vertigo never punctured the vale, a long-lost entry into the night. Be a pleasure, it will alight.

Byron – are you the one we are looking for? Are you the one who needs nothing less than the all of it? There is a half chance in the wind that tarries no whisper. And here where the noise does not recede, a lingering embrace. Come now, we must away.

Forests that do not stop. A flag in the ground that labours for hours. What we see when we come to it is not more than the drowning of deliverance. A station in the middle of nowhere. What we thought was the way home. What we thought.

Byron – Your Mary Chaworth. You were deeply infatuated with her, but she was for another. After you had become famous, and her relationship had broken down, she contacted you! The noise in the abbey does not sink.

Like another thing, masts of a wild sea. Don't come too close, there is never enough time. Shall we beat a hasty drum? Shall we treasure up the rainbow, and know it to be a thing of utmost beauty. We can only go forward. Forward it is.

Byron – a lingering shadow, that has as its peak the raining of a windswept pass. And then, just to tell a story, we adventure on the traipsing just to see what we can see. Is there some-thing more? Is there something we must nestle into?

Having a fair run of it, the night will not relinquish the daylight, not for a second. And here, where the show is of the might and timbre, there comes a mill-stone that knows which way to turn. A light in the day – a semblance into the marrow.

Byron – Causing nothing to suddenly turn, the very voice inside us is not what we expect. Can there be a time for victories? A time for shortcomings? What is this feeling we have? Is it in the sway of it? Is it in the way of it? We will see.

Another way to slide. New hands and soluble feet. Can we ever believe in the rest of it – we must. And then without a thought nor care, we send ourselves longing.

Byron – up against it, we do not tether. There are fires that do not traipse. There are wander-ings that have as their safety the well-wishes of an age. Forego the noise we make, it will not enliven the scene. Heart in for a while – no, forever.

And then, with thoughts of conscious need, there is a stable door that heralds only dice, and the wandering of autumnal desire. Feel the last hope of a stranger, she will be like never be-fore. I am wanting to sense something else. Do not be afraid.

Byron – an assiduous approach, that cast no strength, no strength to bloom. What is this that harks upon entry? Is it the wind, that blows in gale? That grows in stature like the newly found? Byron, are you with us, or against the rail? We are there.

Forever restless, forever mighty. Your life knows how to sing the earth unto. There is like an angel in need, and that is best way of explaining it. There will come a time when the lopsided in us will rally. And here, we come again – why not now?

Byron – On to Cambridge. You kept a tame bear in your rooms. There was a hark for a ranger – despite all compass. There is now a willow in the way, the way of it. Hope, hope for a minute, that runs in time to the dismal and the like. We have come.

There is a lineage that knows only of the bombastic. And here where timings jingle, and the abrasions never stay, I have felt a way forward. What is left, is never astray, what has come forth is like the wind. There is nothing here. Nothing to remember.

Byron – It is like a holler, that knows how the steam is driven. It is like a dance – a dance ma-cabre. And then, despite acceptances, there comes a time to believe once again. What have we thought, but all that is? What have we salvaged? – Yes.

Calling again for that sound from the mist, we will come bent on something special. Are you the tripartite that never lingers? Is this what it takes? Is the motion of the wind the sound of greater things? Do not be shy, faces come. Come and then go.

Byron – do you whisper in the dark? Is this the feeling of it? Can we signal again so that our signal can be seen? I am with you, man of measures. I see your strength, and know the blood in you to be drained from silk. Do not cry, it will only come.

Foregoing, and the blistering of steel. Is there more than this? Is time a repartee to the stars? We will come again, in new forms and new ways to be. Standing firm, we cannot belittle here. Standing firm, the stove does not sink. I will know things.

Byron – is yours of the essence? Is the feeling you have now for the dream? I am one to won-der, and set bulls in motion. Do not feel your way slowly, at pace is the only speed in question. I have thought never to ruffle feathers – but I will.

There is only one thing we need, and that is the bark of a mystical tree. This bark gives life, as it gives soul. And then,

without fear, we come forward, such that the weather heeds
no steel. We move in that direction, only for the trembling.

Byron – Cambridge, you kept horses and a carriage People
were only too ready to lend you money, which kept you
tethered for years to come. At least you used your carriage
to see plays in London. Forever in the middle of things. Rest.

Hanging on, by the nearest thread. I cannot see the way
forward. Wait, hang on, there it is – a pinprick in the clouds –
forward, and abouts, we will see things clearly now. There is
always a way forward, always, and then around, and
through.

Byron – do you love, still? Are you fashioned in silk? Do the
times never change? I have a wanting that retreats nowhere.
Be the thing that shines, and yours is a never-ending
wonder-land. Be the tempest, and yours will be greatness.

I have a need to find the same way again. And here, where
the shallows are enough to won-der, there will come a levity,
that launches as it cries. I will sense something new, before
we have landed. Don't be dismissive, something harrows as
it renews.

Byron – I have seen you, before the glade. There is a nice
fellow waiting to see you. Can we surprise the mass, but
maybe for a second? There is life amongst these hills, and a
readiness to redress. Cancel all fine boutiques, there is a
long haul now.

The sense we have to continue is not what we had thought
of. But then, there is love in the air. Do not breathe here,
there is a time for that, and a time for nothing. What is it that
we ape for? Is it the wind? The slope, and the concourse?

Byron

Byron – is this the way to proceed? Have we lost the compass, only to follow the moon? There is something else we must consider, and it is like the cascade of the waterfall. There is a temptation to jump in, and see the well-wishes.

To gather up life, and send those that see to the outer edge. There will be time enough. I hold your hand, and know your palms to be simple. We must not languish, maybe only for a time, and then – yes, and then – we will know it.

Byron -Those close to you knew your plight. And then, a hope that things would be in the as-cension. Never changing, always seeing. The topmost of the world – there are things that do not splinter. Be a weathering, what's more, and then some.

Trickling down, the weather invites. Invites stories of sea lost realms. Do not be careful here, we must tread vigorously where we go. There is never a heart where the soul will follow. And here, where we love to be, a new sanction, ready to give.

Byron – The grand tour. Hobhouse kept the diary, and off you went. Never looking back, or forwards for the that matter. The tail lingers in the sun. Where the dutiful and the blind both see as clearly as each other. Do not stride, you will win.

As envisaged, a welling up of time. Be the guiding buoy, and all that you see will be yours. A keeper's mess. There are shoulders here that reckon in the light. Can't we simply be, like we used to? There is enough to keep us company. We will see.

Byron – have you seen the half of it? Have you listened to the dawn, and followed her there? There is more to this adventure than is waiting to be seen. Byron, can you wait until all is ac-counted for? Be wonderous, we know you can be.

What is left of our ease? What of the tribulations of an age? To be the rest in sorrowful composure. Be what we can see. Be the victory in the march, and sense will come of nonsense. The distance I see myself travelling cannot be yours, Byron.

Byron – do you swim again, passed the Hellespont? Is this your victory post? Your time to shine, in amongst the harrows. Be what comes next? There will be time. Time to be, what's more time to live. Do not be ashamed, we will make it.

Claw back at will. Claw the dangers which lurk. Do not swing the standard, there will only be a noise. This is part of our enterprise, to reach, and settle forth. Jumping with abandon. The hysteria of feelings does not select a willing dream.

Byron – A clever design, that has no width. More than a measure, we will not seal the place. In the midst of it, a cooling grace. I have felt the times pass, and have felt the ginger gap, both without a tear. But now, we must remember. We will.

And then, side and front, the troubadour of our epoch says, with a certain finality, 'yes this is it'. Do not wonder here, there can be no time. I have said before that the rose water is the only thing that knows how the distance works. This will be enough.

Byron

Byron – are you the one not to flinch? Are you the one to be steady on the stage? Is this what it takes, takes to flesh out the bottom of it. We will know our rambling mass. But what have we seen, that can only be seen twice? We will come.

A mischief that has no herald. A dawn that has the rite of spring. Can we sense what has come? Is this what we should deliberate on? I will come up only for air. And then maybe not. I chose to waver in colours, waver in the moon and its shadows.

Byron – Upon your return from your tour, you composed your long poem, Childe Harold. Its publication saw you instantly famous. English society opened its doors to you. And then, with aplomb, seizing what is best, in the twilight.

Furtive, and reminiscent of. There is never anything to round away. And here, where we find ourselves anew, there is a likeness to the clouds. Do not be shy, we will only send our selves without reply. And, as in now, do not slumber too long – we will see.

Byron – There is here a place to dream, and a place to live. What have we said, but all that is? There is an eclipse that will not away. And then, with an amount bravado that needs no saving, we will send ourselves again into the mist, and then away.

Listen intently. Just as the warrior survives the day, just as the wave survives the sea, there is a new type of landing. And that, will also see us survive, unto the next, unto the day. What of our next recourse? What of the daylight in between?

Byron – are you one to see the hemisphere directly? Are you one to douse the embers? Is this where we come for the side of things – you have another lover, I ask your courtesy, is she in-trepid as are you? I sense a companionship. In love.

There are things we do not understand. There are lights we cannot see. And here, where things often become lost, we have found something very worthwhile. And that is where things are found, in the very middle of the valley. We will not stop.

Byron – Is this your temporality which you show me? Is this the land under your feel? Is this what we have come for, never to see again? I am utmost at your guard. I am here, for winding through the tempest. I am spoken for, to distance and to shire.

Forgetting, and never saying less. I wander, and then wonder. I am entrenched in snow. Winter is upon us, in wary, and in sundry. Clash with fits of raven feather. I have a belief in myself again. Classical singularity. Nothing else helps.

Byron – It is like the mistress of time. It is like the desert steps, the call unto the way of things. I have climbed several mountains to be here, and more I will climb. There is a caustic embrace that tarries forward into the night-time.

Close to the centre of things, there is a sound. Close to the heart of things, there is a sight. And then, when we are there, a wisp of smoke, and they are gone. Come let us be ecstatic, as only we can be. There are things to savour, and things to let go of.

Byron – are you the one to live? Is this the fashion of the day? We can see ourselves in amongst it again? I will not fathom more. I will not fathom less. Come to the startling point, there will be a catch. I hope you are well, is what I would say.

Forget the new stone, it does not see. It is only here to sit, and this, in distinct moments. Come and see your remedy, it has no division, nor quarter. Give us the way of things, we are here to do the bidding of time. And without care, crescendo.

Byron – are you not the one to speak in tones of dried wood? Does your daughter listen to the skies? Is this what we mean when we say, yes it is not gone. Be a parlance to a strange lan-guage, and that language with multiply evenly.

A washing gaze that has as its fault-line that never before seen newness of a fate driven steed. What we have come to see, is not the tempest in the wind – that we have seen before. What we have come to see, is life itself, in its very first stages.

Byron – Do you come for fresh fish, Byron? Is this what the hands of neverness have never know. There is in the laughter of this fish monger, a new type sound. I am one to envisaged a town in harvest, where the dusk light shines on woolly meter.

A sentence we can never speak of. It is here, and we must give it a wide birth. And then, with-out a sense of this or that, we come for something more, and overnight, something old, some-thing in the rain water perhaps? We can never tell.

Byron – do you have for friendship all the gulls of winter wills? Is this the time it takes? Do we send our feeling with us to the wall of township? I have now known nothing else. And here, we strike forth again. In search of what? Everything.

Taking a course of action that is warranted. Seeing something more than the dawn. And here, folly on the waves, folly on the shore. There is a now a chance to break from the water, and see the ounces flag in new accomplishment. We will come.

Byron – Do you sail to places unknown? Do you give what is not in store? Feeling comes to us, but what do we do with it? Is your adventure mounting, seething in realms untold? Is this what we do? Is this what we say? Come, much awaits.

There is a catch, that has no winter feel. And when we come, we come to gather the petals of the rose that has won its way through. Do not treasure anything more, we have the arborist here. There comes a sound that has no recourse to the moon.

Byron – are you one to give the scene a wide birth? Are you one to say things never come in threes? There is still something we must not miss. There is a migration to the sky that has as its course the temptation to do as small as we can.

Gaining in momentum, the trees herald new times to share with friends. What are these times? What are the arcs of breathing that we all do to stay alive? Such is their bounty, such is their wrath. We will come again to see new friends.

Byron – What is this I see you fathom? Is it the bottom, or the top? Is this where we know where to go? Byron, are you now the cascading of the waterfall? Images, and flashes of imag-es. We will not curtail their effect. A narrowness, we must away.

Byron

What have we thought, but everything? What have we sensed, but top-most greetings? I will have it no other way, to catch on feathers unused. There is a template that has as its mould the whispering of fate.

Byron – are you the one to stand still? Or are you in flight for things to come? I have never felt the way before, but this is how it goes. I am one to see things in due course. But what is the blistering compass to send for? I am sure of many things.

Come now, we have more than the ocean to lavish – lavish upon and through. There are now things that have as their anchor a sort of chain, one that listens on to milk and honey. There are times to be in the knowing, and times to be still.

Byron – The eclipse knows the round, as the sun knows its place. But what of us, in times of rancour, and of sleep? There is more to this equation than the dunes of winter solstice come for. You are there, where we all are. You are there.

A little more of the landing on thin air, and less of the beating down on sons of antipodean grace. There is here something we must not forget. And what is that, that we cannot see from any point to any point. A rustic charm pervades the scene.

Byron – Lots to see, and lots to feel. There is now a semblance of the catching of things, that has as its bellows the nuance of a thousand dreams. Be the way we see, and there will more than enough to answer. Come, and be away.

I will never see the sands again just like this. There is a listening that has only ripeness down to the base. I am like something else. Something else in the trees. I will not let go, not even for the breeze. Come and let sense prevail.

Byron – A sense we have that the laughter we hear is like a forge in autumn. There can only be the way of things, and then the very fibres of our lives will come to be settled. What is more, certainty, will guide the way. And yes, in between.

A season beyond another. There is a chance to be on time, but time for what? I will not give the likelihood of another song. Come now, the borders are auspicious. What have we given, that has not turned back? I will gather the remnants before me.

Byron – are you the one to manage the load? Are you the one to settle forth, and have the ring of remembrance squarely between your feet? There is something here we do not understand. It beats as the drum of an old lesson.

And yes, there is a road ahead, one that we have not travailed through. Come and settle into arms. Come and be that thing that does not stop. There are ropes here. Ropes to guide the unwary. Have a fully engaged intent, and then smile.

Byron – Catching the sight of it, I am assured that the kindness of the place will see us through. Be a formative care, and what will beckon will start an age. There is more here than the world can forget. This much is clear to us.

Helping something that is amiss. Being true to the sense of it. Upholding so much. There is the window and the lyre bird. I have not thought to do this on my own. The compunction is here, but what of the bravery?

Byron

Byron – do you love, here and again? Is yours the typeset in regalia? Do you see yourself again? I am want to like what I see - only because we know ourselves to be these sorts of people, who listen intently through to the end of things.

Come and see the way back from the abyss. There is nothing in the way of it. Be the tremor stone to our vagaries. There will come a time for steeling ourselves against the tide. I have not shown you the way forward. I have not.

Byron – There comes a found object in the sea. It is like the invigoration of the horizon. Are you one to see it, Byron? And then, without the message to keep fawning, we love that which is, and that which is not.

Fetching things from below. Feeling as if we are a candle in the night. Being treasured, like a fanfare. There is nothing left to do. But one thing, and that is all. We have here the barometer of an epoch. Sense beyond the nonsense.

Byron – did you creep, as another would crawl. Do you send the likes of it down the alleyway that has a life to live, and a settling that does not divide? You are here with me Byron. You are here, where the road leads to depth, and to life.

A little bit at a time, we come for the limit of things. And here, where nothing sleeps, there re-mains a doing that has a heart as well as is whole. There bridges a gap in the breathes of two proteges as they listen once again.

Byron – Grasping tight, we will come to gather all motion. Is this what we know to be true? By-ron, are you the one to be as the invective, for all our might and tether? There is a place, that counters all this. It is inside us. We must look.

Paul Fearne

A gap in the film of things. We know ourselves to be in unison with so much. There can only be one thing to see, and we have seen it. Be the touch stone at the wishing well. Yes, we have no need of the rest of it. We will be as we like.

Byron – What is the cost of life upon us? The world and things lived through? There is a task no harder, no harder than the wings of fashion-hood. And then, the unknown levity sees us through. A laughter that rings in our ears, and through our souls.

The tour that beckons. What more is fate? I have here in my hands all that is. I wish to find more in the wind. There is like a force of nature in between these wings. I will not love until I leave. There is a place. There is a place. We will find it.

Byron – Are you the one to speak? Speak of harrowing tides? I have felt the trembling from above. To have made it through, I beckon you come. And here, where rest is like the garb it-self. There is a time to sail away. Yes.

A sort of adhesion to the height of it, pulls us through. And then, without the conscious deliv-ery of the seam, there lingers a solemn rite. And here, where we dream that solemn dream, the last in a series. We douse ourselves in water.

Byron – Is this the way we are needed, through repartee, and time itself. I cannot commit to the well, abouts. There is something more here, and something across. There is a tempest, out of site, readying itself for the flight.

The call, it reckons, your Greece, my grace. And there, where the timepiece is like a shallow log, there comes a new form to galvanise by. A shower in the rain. This much will hold us. This much will tally us away to greater nights.

Byron – happening across the sky. A burst of cloud, then the moon. We can't see which is which. But here, where the twilight never renounces, there is like a settling in, a settling in for something more. Do we have what it takes?

There is gumption here. Solidly arriving, before anything else. I am like the sustenance of all out spring. Do not settle, there is nothing to sleep on here. And then, when we least expect, a rattling that has as its aperture the night sky.

Byron – seeing how things are. Seeing the fob watch at the altar. Doing what is best. Trudging through, and seeing how things go. There can never be a time like this. There can only be what is left. And here, where the moisture defies, a schism.

Hopelessly adrift in a sea of another man's making. There is the time it takes. There is a sal-vageable equation. Never coming to see things as clearly as this. What is it that we seek? What is it that is sought for? What is it that we need?

Byron – are you aware of the night? Are you aware of the new soul that governs old things? There is something like a talisman that guides the weary. Do not yawn here, the distance never matters. And then, overcoming every obstacle. Precisely.

Catching on fire, due north, has the incumbency we seek. And then, when we are more wary that a troupe of soldiers in the cold, there is a mattress beyond the sail. Are we the one's to disband the travail of things? We will come, I say.

Byron – Are you here for us? Is your time, our desire? Can we simply be, be in amongst is all? I love the stern fact of it, the thing that reaches the daylight, and then knows the returning hawk. Never say swim – Sorry, always say swim.

A feather at the start of things. A rapier in between things. We have come to always miss. And then, when the hand of redemption rattles, we will know where to go. Hand over foot, and nary a hopeful beat. Come for this, and it will be still.

Byron – is this where we seek you, in the motion of mighty tropes? Do not preclude the truth. Do not be where we are not. All the while thinking, a heart in September. I have found no turn to fashion. I have no life to encompass. We will not fall.

A clover in the wind. A smell of something fresh. Do you tell of land unbidden? Do you range forth in a temporal mode? There is a sense in all of this. A sense to gather the rose petals. I have found something new. I have found something in between.

Byron – do you delight in feathers of after year? Is this where we seek, in patterns of remiss, patterns of partaking? I have never seen you like this, rainbow in silk. There is something we should try. Something we should at least try. Come.

I have seen the utmost. I have seen it clearly. And then, without foibles, a landing, that tethers our ship to the stability of land. We will come again, on land as in water. There is like a new delivery for the top most of us. Do not doubt.

Byron – fashioning a loop in the sail. Never once missing a temperance. Come and be alive to it all. Come and be that which cannot falter. Forging ahead, and through. Never once with a remiss at heart. I have seen the fixity of the call.

Byron

Coming close, we see the need to launch. And then, when the lead lighting rumbles by, there is something else we must remember. I have seen the way through, and it is marvellous. We should all see it. Give us what is left. Yes. What is left.

Byron – there is a lake. Around this lake, there are shores. On these shores, at the packaging of vice-royal desires. Do not come back here. We must not swim the length, except for you By-ron, you can swim any length you like.

The mixture of sounds on painted glass. There is no time like this. No time like now. Come and see ourselves between showers. There is a like mindedness that comes in regal splendour, do not tarry, it is the way. Come now, we must away.

Byron – do you arch your feet. Do you say to those amongst it, steady on? Have you the way inside you. Come close to me now, I have the witness of the trees. There is now a time to har-row, and a time to rest in ease. I am one not to say.

The glare, glare from the sun, steels the light for something more. Do we see things one more time? Do we have at our disposal a feathering that does not lie. I am the one who seeks in times of array. Do not be the well, its coins are for the bottom.

Byron – a love lost, and then regained. Are we transposing the gulf between us? Are we seen in times of victory, in time of solitude? There is a chance at the windswept, and the noise. I love what I see. And I see you, Byron. Come and be away.

Paul Fearne

Whispered regret, and times of ancient past. There is a likelihood of milk to rattle bones. I am the one to see things through. And here where the dance is for the forager, I have it in mind to do as I please. Come now, a new type of sound.

Byron – love the one you have. I will nestle in, to see things pass. And here where the invigoration is at a height, there comes something new – something to hold us in sway, and then back again. I will not linger. I will say it again, I will not linger.

A fist, a fist that is unclenched. And now, we see more, more than is possible. I will be the one to carry on. I will not stop, for anything. And now, the dirge is like a hollowing. There comes a direction, which way to go. This much will save us.

Byron – are you the way back, as the way forward? Is this which way we should go? I have seen something of strident care in the limbs of every traveller who has come out of the rain. Must we stay, before time? I come for you Byron. In amidst.

Gaining in confidence, the last of the Tsars takes his position in front of us. And then, without fault, nor reason to rhyme, there comes a salutation, and a need to breathe that one last breath. We come now to the palace of the wisdom. We touch it.

Byron – There are places we cannot go. There are places we can wander through. And then there is home. Have no stance to stay, nor understanding to deliver. And when we come again, we come for the test of strength, that barrels as it treats

Coursing through unseen, we carry our load in tempest like procession. And then, when the likelihood of succession is paramount, we say, in any language we like, we say a strict 'com-miseration'. There are nuances to once again be.

Byron – I sense your tingling. Only at special moments are you like this. I come for your agree-ance. And in that, we see the clime for what it is – just that, a gaining of height. I will come to you later, when my legs are less saw. Yes, anon

Strictly speaking, there is nothing like this. Nothing like the beck and call of fate, as she wash-es us against the wall of a spritely fan dance. I have come for something similar. I have come though the translate this into new languages, and old.

Byron – is this your fare? The in between of fanfare, that has no delicacy like the movement of old bones, and new hearts. I have a mind to come back again. Will you be one to drag me back. I have found a way, like a moisture in the window.

Catching the last of it. Giving notice to the weary. I must not be dishevelled. But of course, I will be. There is something delayed, that has not been thought of for a thousand years. And here, where things standstill, I will come to you.

Byron – are you the one to say when? Is this what you have encountered, a wall within a wall? Do you say, okay, to the mount and the motion? Is this where we know things to be? I have one more banner, it says rise for you. And then.

There are places that guard no lassitude. There is not a semblance to the night. I have come a thousand miles, to see what all the fuss is about. There are times in amongst it that delivers of the furthest time. We will see it fresh.

Byron – is this your final aplomb? Is this the way forward, through an about? I have heard it said, that when the wind blows, it blows in threes. Is this the truth of it? Can we startle the masses with a new try at the night? And here, a chance again.

Byron – A little bit of sunshine to settle into things. There, in the middle of it all, likeness settles the scene. Every word is accounted for, every word a dream. I have not seen the dandelion delay in more than a blue aeon. We will come again.

Forgetting where we linger. Forgetting where the road turns. I am here, here like never before. I have a sense of things that treads no domain, and no inkling to fire, nor ice. I am a believer in you, the way of things.

Byron – there is a likeminded engagement that silks in reams, that has is the foyer, a new tree, and a new marriage. And when we come, we come in spirals untold. And then, without thought, nor care, a rambling mass that rumbles as it retorts.

Forcing the rug to sheds its tears. There is now a time once again to take up the banister, and have our scars removed, and have them placed with the bounds of time. Do this once for us, we will be thankful like the wind in autumn embrace.

Byron – Fixing the map, to hear our silence. There is more to it than that. There is more to the sound of things than we give the land. And here, where we cannot placate the moon, there is a sound that has no voice – no centre to find.

The eagle and the lyre bird have come full circle. And here where the mischief of the night is tamed in golems of string, there tempers a new and mighty noise. I have found this sound be-fore, but only once. I know it to be good, and indeed not remiss.

Byron

Byron – there is more time than we can speculate. More time than arborist, has at will. And then, the inarticulate. What do you say, when saying is the lead of knowledge? There can be only one sort of feeling. And we must feel it.

Conscious of the way through. We battle the night as if we had never seen the stars. Do not be the charging, for your horse will belittle the domain. Come and have a new story, one that will be half of what is needed. I am the single to your multiple.

Byron – is this you? Is this the way to go? I have not seen the sun. I have only felt its presence. But what of this, and surely? There is like a wind at my side. There is something more also. I do not know what. But that is okay. Forthwith.

And then, without a single second of recalcitrance, there lives and breathes one to study the aptness of things. I have not seen the drive, in likeness of the rest, but that is okay. I sense a new domain, one yet to be traversed. Come now, we must away.

Byron – Are you the one to savour things? Is this what it takes, to jump straight in, and never carry forward. This is what we say when times are at ease, and we are at liberty not to bite back. I hear the trumpet - it absconds. We will fight for it.

Without thought, nor care, the tendrils of love fashion themselves a new boat to sail by. And here where the wind is deep, there claws a sense at new found dreams. I will not hang on to the tethers that bind – no more will I see them flutter.

Byron – a sort of victory march, that belittles nothing as it comes forward in harnessing mass. I have never felt the tragedy of the sky one to hold on to the dance of light – from this rooftop to the next. There are things we must not martyr. Yes.

And now, when all is quiet, a peculiar sense that overcomes us. It is the sense of an all or nothing belief in things. A sense that the carrying of weight will drive us forward, like pinions on high winds. There is more to life, or is there?

Byron – is yours the multitude, the number that sings in choral applause? Is yours the way of things that has no way? Is this the top of all things. I wonder sometimes at the use and parsi-mony of the message – a missive that has only sound to greet us.

The conch shell on the beach. Its repartee is one of hardship, and of grace. There is a mois-ture in the wind, but that is not all. There is a sort of playfulness that doesn't let go. When we are on a long journey, this becomes apparent. Lead on.

Byron – do your legs curl with night when you have undergone your starvation diets? When did you say your hour of need was? Do we say your graces in the dead of night? A land less moved by. Less sought for, but now, much more.

Gaining in ground, so that the maxim doesn't shirk belief in hours of trouble. There can be the smallest thing, and then, the largest thing. And then no-thing worth a thing. Come now, do not flinch. The tide upon us, but what next?

Byron – and then, without the cause to be, there climbs up the rail, a sempiternal belief. What is this thing? It is the

gateway to the nuanced and the placated. We have
witnessed so much, that to see this chamber of the now,
does not belie.

Carry on, but do not cry. Not in my earshot. Do not wish, and
then run. There are pleasures before the ruin. I have sent
my missive back a yard or two. And here, where the times
give way to shadows, we lie again in repose. Here, and
here, alone.

Byron – do you see yourself in the strictest silk? Does the
day have something for you, and you alone? I am luckiest in
the way. I see things that are not for this world. And then, a
cata-comb to rest with. We see when things are dull. This
much is true.

A hazard we cannot see. A traipsing that raises the
challenge. And then, despite ourselves, wonder, and the
indisposed of. Do not have the kite fly too high. We need it
here. But gives us the time? Is it the joy and grandeur of the
such-ways?

Byron – are you ready? Is your soul entwined in yesterdays?
There is like a thin film here – a film that keeps the water
attuned. Be the listening we do, and you will forever have a
saviour. And then without things ahead, what do we do,
despite?

Verily and without the need to say so. There is a canvas
foretold. And here, there comes a night-time without the
mystery rehearsed. And now we sit, and have the chambers
flushed to the right, and to the left. Come what may, we will
see.

Byron – is yours a time for temperance? Or a feat for the
senses? I can tell you, there is noth-ing like the later, but

why do we say that, when the laughter we hear is of lovers
and their polish. Byron this is you. Why not come?

And here, where the festivities are sparse, there comes a
legion of the night to dwell on ancient seas. We cannot feel
the rapidity, that does not belong to us. We cannot
understand the way forward, when the way back is blocked.
Be true.

Byron – are you with us in guise as in silk? Do you settle in
charms of maiden flower? Is this what we say, when the
saying is all aloft? Do not be the one to fall, it does not suit
you. The chances are like fish gills that seem never to rise.

Forests and the gloom of night. Forests and the shine of the
day. There is a mystery to it all. A mystery that has no
strength, nor time to reckon. What more can we say? But we
must in times of fortune as in times of grey. Do not sing for
us. We will follow.

Byron – the trudging up slopes of snow, slopes of tenor.
There are things here that have as their vice, the whispering
of shadows rent. And then, without a conceivable notion, the
heart strings are left pounding, and left holding themselves
back.

Gauging the spring, gauging it for all it is worth. There is a
tendency to be what may. And here, where the noise does
not travel, there is a vestibule that seeks no fear, and
harnesses no platform. Come and be the one untethered.
We must sleep.

Byron – Like in times of distress, there are broader missions
to encounter. Broader things to once again feel. Do not send
the way of it through the hills, for, in themselves, they are
noth-ing. We are through, and beyond. Be still.

Byron

The distaste we have for nothing that raises the bar, is for something else entirely. The weak-ness of the shrew is our weakness, the strength of the crow, our strength. Come back to us, we can see the way.

Byron – seething in the mist, you come. Your fellow travellers are like eyes on silk. The whis-pered tenure of the thoroughfare is enough to bind. Do you know what the difference is, be-tween this and that? There are chances at the remiss.

A bottomless juncture, that wills itself on. There are tethers that have no delight, but some that do. The sense we have that the right is a fight. Come and be the sorrow for times gone by, and then, when we least expect, a new found commiseration.

Byron – There is here more spread than on the shirt of a sailor. Come and witness the dive of two and two, and you will march the deadly march of the keeper, the keeper of hearts. I am one to believe in things. And then, with nothing else.

Like this thing, that wheels and chugs, there is cause to hear again, and a chance to be intrepid. The cause of our energy is simply to be, and be standing. That is the secret to it. There is hope amongst the trees, hope we saw coming.

Byron – The sentience in the night, a thing that heralds deep, is more than hearts beat. And then, a lonely embrace, that leaves the stars pounding with vied for tenacity. And then, a love, one that sooths the lassitude of the soul.

Come and be a passion here, one that sees as it runs. We have fought for the sight of it, and then listening deeply, we come to our own impasse. There is a new found wandering, that has as its fit, the noise of nightly meanders. Reckon with.

Byron – the test of it is in the park. The test of it is in the cobblestones. Yes I have seen the way, it is hard. Do not tremble at the opening, there is a sense that I have the kings and queens of knowledge help bundle the way. True and true.

The living we do at the best of times, is enough to solidly fix our breath on ilk of clay, ilk of stay. And then, when the trees are still, and the long lost has its fire, there is a new wandering through times of pure-ness, and times of abandon.

Byron – are you the one to leave in oak, leave in desire. Can we see the simplicity in the reams of it, without recall, without detestation? And there stands the beauty of it, Byron. There stands the wind of, and that does not bother us. We are here to settle.

Walking in winter with no boots on, there is a certain elongation that does not mist, as might does not hiss. Come in strange lines, and un-heard of values. There, in the distance, some-thing to behold. What is that? We will never see, not hear it.

Byron – A little of the upside, is all that keeps me afloat. And then when you come, you come to please. Do not feel so threatened as you do now. And in this is the world at large. And knowledge of the turning of things, is imagined.

Byron

Having no more than a kettle in which to boil the water. I see what is drowning, and attempt to take it with me. There is something in the way of, something that tenders, as it disfigures. I swim to cast no inclusions. And there without care, a new bear.

Byron – Much intrigued, and much belittled. The House of Lords, a new throw. What is more, delectation to you. Never see to way through. It is not for us, nor for the wind. I have come for something new, to cast a pall over – and then, it is here.

Catching the light of it, before in darkens. Never once seen in the way of it. Come, and do not splendour. Come, and come again, we will be with you, and with you always. The sharpness of the sun bears no resemblance to the daylight here.

Byron – do you sense the way to be, and be strong? Is this what we do to have a life, in amongst it all? There, composure. And there, long footfalls. We sense a feeling that is to come, and one that is yet to come. Do the sense of alarm a favour.

Gathering up the petals, and knowing the earth to be a granter. What should we say, when to say belittles the truth? Never conscious of the way of things, we sense our demise in label sweet offerings. Do the best you can, there will be time.

Byron – Geneva, and the Shelley's. Dark wanderings and stable myths. We have a new con-trol, on things, but not hearts. We have the doors to our home strung intransigence. And then, when the falcon sees the terrace, aplomb.

Picking at littered rocks. And then, without the need to be anymore, I rise myself to see again. That is all I can do. And then, then the noise of the bottom creeks into life, here will be a thing that has not been touched. That much is assured.

Byron - Coming up the rear, but seeing a line in the sand and going for it. We have done nothing but spilt white in the trees, and then, held it for more than a minute. We are the ones to banish the storey teller to the upmost reaches.

Conscious of the need to be, we now hold our fate aloft, and see what the future says. There is a glimpse and a nod, and more of the same. We are there, and the same is, yes, more of the same. It is ours to see forth. Come, now.

Byron – An ancient belief, lies for you Byron. It is here to wonder in silk, and pass in times of trial and invigoration. Do not sense anything more, anything more than can be stabled. There is now civility from all quarters.

A sort of salience that does not diminish. A listening that never wavers. I hear you now, in the mist of it. And then, wildfire, and a touch of a salt on the breeze. There is here, now, a se-quence of events, that belittles the mainstay, only for a while.

Byron – Augusta, where are you? A feather that allows no temperament. A king fisher that marries in arcs of red and blue. There is a sound here, one that allows only mischief to be born. Come know, we must not reflect, we must simply do.

Gaining an inch, by taking a mile. That is life sometimes in amongst the trees. Do not feather the time piece with lards of grey. There is now, a weathering that impedes not the sand that it is gained upon. Have the last of it, we will see how it is.

Byron – And now, come and be a part of the grey, as to stay is never enough. I feel you in the winter months – your cold is like ice. Your drive is like the dawn's. And here, where the noise is at its peak, a whole world emerges.

A constant surprise that knows only how to be. And then, with the narrowness in between, there comes a trace that does not diminish. Herald to the stark, I hear you say. There is some-thing more besides. Can you be placated, to never leave?

Byron – Like wisdom, but only around the garden bed. Like the far cry, but only when we choose it. For the need we all have, to live life in regards. Annabella – did you find him there, eventually? There is a noise that beckons no ghost.

A well-spring that harks no hawk. Be that as it may, a tributary to the stars of the night sky. There is a liking of rubble, where water once was. And here, where the kindling is like the moon, there shines neither this nor that. Be sure.

Byron – are you the one to laugh and play? Is this what you do to say what's what. There is a belief in the steel of things, that carries the weight of neverness. And here, where the noxious and the foibled rings in our ears, we come for the tethers.

There can be nothing left of this. Nothing that is felt in simplest harmony. And here, where the motion of the spheres approximates the wind of the rainbow, there comes a blowing within that erases the tempest on the spot. Do not climb here, we can't.

Byron – are you the one to see the bastion for the bridge of it? Do you calculate a further sound in amongst it? There is time enough, to see and hear. And then, a caution in the wind. There is a sign that reads only too well. We will find it.

Conscious of the moon, we see the furthering of what lies ahead. Is there a touch of trepidation here, that mars itself in the flight of birds across the sky? And then a new wonder, that has no decision, nor harrow to bolt on tightly. Come for the show.

Byron – Milan, and the opera. We see you sample on past, and know the tide is not for the rousing. And here, a fault is found, much vaunted and much maligned. There can only be the things which bight. We will see the way of it. And then, utmost.

The gathering of the stars. The lingering of mass like territory. And then, a truism, that rings true. Have we the sense of it amongst the best, amongst the most, and amongst the continua-tion. Clouded, and then passed. Ricochet and most.

Byron – Is this the chance I have – to see amongst it, to see my journey in full, and revel in it? I hope so, but as all things, we will see. Imagine that – imagine the hills are there. Imagine the time to come, it all its repartee. Yes, fine.

Wishing for the ocean, and its spray. Wishing for the humility to come next. Wishing for us, together, wishing for that, that which moves the rays. I can have all this, once I have shed a tear for the past, and know it to be a thing worth counting.

Byron – Venice, Carnival – do you remember? Is the past inside you too? The motion in in-crease is increasing. There is a faun due east from here. It beckons the light from the candle, and sees what is never sought. We will consider everything.

The whispers in the dark. The mounting of new things on the wall. The distance that never speaks. I have found a way, but do not wish to speak of it. I have found the chance to read through my blindness. And that is a blessing in halves.

Byron – having you close. Knowing full well your armoury, and how it works. My last book was of that ilk. But don't dispel myths until they are given. There is a chance to really be here, in many senses of the word. A really here we will come.

Catching the rhyme before it is rehearsed. Being more pleasant than before. Having the switch come to the table. And then we figure it out for ourselves, and know that the arc is one of sublime beauty. Do not hesitate, the shine will come through.

Byron – Are you to say, how many others have vied for your affection? There is nothing else, apart from this. And here, where we lay with full intent – full intents and purposes, we come again, like a swallow in the mist. We will be.

Gaining a reputation, we see what is next. And what we have is the tapestry of twilight. And then, the fashion of things is to come again, and then never leave. I am the truth of it, as we are its bards. We can catch the rain if we choose.

Byron – there are things that have no vault, and things that do. And here, where the wasteland is removed once again, there comes a chalice that hides all the invectives. The invectives for what? Homeward, and upward, bound.

Mission through, mission deep, there are plans for the wealth of nationhood. And then, when the demise of ceilings holds us still, we will fathom the likelihood of change, and then know the way even deeper. Chance, and the parlance for it.

Byron – a sound we have yet to hear, is with you Byron. And thanks to it, we may live again. Reading about your life, we come to understand what we are doing better. And that much is true. The story continues, and unfolds in new ways.

Breaking fast, the being of all passion does not impede, but only resonates from within. The whispering of deep regret comes, but we fight for more than life itself. There is a cacophony, that inches forward, and know nothing of the maligned.

Byron – In Venice, you had a mistress. And the little of not knowing receded, and the task of centre-hood remained. And then with the arc solemn, there was a twine, a twine to bind all else. A mainstay, and the chance to shine.

According what is great, to what is ample. And here, where we love to sell our wares, attention doubles, and weaves in amongst the lowest ebb. Be here, my chosen view. Be here where we should be, and here where we love to be.

Byron – Let the vase stay as it should. Let the accoutrement settle all wagers. Hang on softly, there is more to say. We are the ones to see through the water of life. And then, like a red rose, the marching comes in stow, and never without.

Left in the charcoal of the beginning of things. There is a sort of penance that one must go through. One must sever ties with the semblance, and have rattle through your bones.

Byron

There is like the noon sun, the only thing we can keep company with.

Byron – The message from the swift is that you may swim again. Swim again, to your hearts content. And here, where the breathless does not sleep, there is a sort of homecoming that transcends as it weeps. Byron, you must – you simply must.

Going again for a nightly stroll – we tender for the race, and know its aegis is long past. And then, without simplest piece of care, we know where we are. And that is where we come from. The circle is complete. And then must derision, but home.

Byron – much known; little really known. And here, where the laughing cauldron speaks its mind, the spits and gurgling rejoice. What is this - says the spot on the wood – a cauldron that speaks its mind – this I find amusing, tell me more.

A cautionary tale – a tale that leads to no hearts, and every piece of sail. The sea, the sea, the might of its beauty, draws beauty seekers from every town that ever was. And then, when we love the sound of things, there comes a new motion.

Byron – Forever delivering the news from new heights – heights out-wayed. There is a new sense to old tidings. New meanings to solemn calls. And then, a slice of the picturesque – which gallery do you go too? Or rather how many?

Having a break, in the master that counts a dozen. There dives with us, a semblance that has with it the sound of breaking. There is never anything we find so heartfelt. And then, with the lips moistened, the heart breaks to another rank all together.

Byron – have a lance at the side of things. Be true, when you are there. And then, as we waltz, we dance to tail the wishing of all four walls. There is like a sound here, that has as it base the sound of peregrine distance. We are left with fire in us.

The conscious laugh, that buries deep. Have no fear of it, there is a paucity of acceptances. I am alive, but I know much. Meaning is not the key, but what is. Yes, what is. Work, and sem-blance of good tidings. Be benevolent, and yours will be.

Byron - your maiden speech in the House of Lords. It can take you many places. And has in-deed. All the way through the denial, through to the misanthrope, through the searching. We have come to serve all purposes. And then, again, through.

Having the spice rack ready, life, is your account with the stars. There is now a never known feeling, a feeling that has its couture the noise of abatement, and the semblance of normalcy. Do not dream here, it is fraught with that which we envisage.

Byron – are you seeking what is left? Is this your way through? I am one to seek the being within? There, yes there, there is where we seek. Turning sides, on the degree of acceptable lesions. Do not come for this. We will come for it.

A sight, and all that is. True style, and the countess of lost causes. And then when we see ourselves anew, we blow half a breath in the right direction, and there, yes there, a new sound, from a new type of bird. One we can see, and hear.

Byron – Is this the time, the time which is right. Do we come to see more, when the door is opened, and the light pierces? We can only say what we know is the way. Treasures and new found hope. I will find you again, and again.

Furthering the belief we have that the sky will not turn. And here, a longer reach, that has as its boundary nothing short of all. Be mellifluous in a solemn age, and yours will be the daylight. You are there, you and I – and then without due course, again.

Byron – a template of the unknown. Something worthy to see. A wonderment that heaves as it gets still. There is a random insouciance that alleviates all. And here, where, a semblance of life draws near, there comes pure folly. Intrepid.

A likelihood that our dreams will come from still higher up. And then, we must let go of things, for that to happen. In the middle of a maelstrom, we can only see past what is next. And then, appeasing the journey, we have the stride about us.

Byron – The last time I saw you, you were in the heat of battle, wrestling with your new manu-script. But that is not something we should tailor to the wind. And here, a furtherance, that delves in times of grey. What's more, we sense accoutrement.

Having the mystery, and having it bright. A foothold in the wind of things. Messing around, with important time-shifts to overcome. There is a delectable nuance that holds us tight.

Come now, we have seen the stunned, let us weep unhindered.

Byron - Pisa, your last stop in Italy before Greece. You brought all your pets. Most encumbered of you. And then, when the dawn flashed before your eyes, it was time to meet your destiny.

Bereft of winter winds, the sort of things we feel are not for the orderly, nor the tempest, but for all that lies in between, and through. The ceiling is now open, and the patterns ours to make. There is little we can see. And yes, enough.

Byron – listening intently. Do you sing for the season's return? Is this where we encounter the cherished aplomb. I am like so much that has the timbre of rain. Do not disregard the forest, it has coals of disinterest. There we are, more in the mist.

Bubbling with desire, the township knows no flagon. And here, where we love to be, a con-scious seed believes once again, that the tempest will come its way for the anchor. Do not di-minish the sound, there is time to be all we need to be.

Byron – are you here with us? Is yours the nightly tumult? Can we see again in times of trou-ble, times of disarray? There is timely sending of ancient wonders. Come now, do not frown. There is ample to come by and to see. Just chose something.

A harrowing approach. Something that lingers, in the heartland. And now in the heart. There is a cautious tale to tell, and one to let go of. The niceties reflect no moon. And here is where we are, most assured. And then, simply let go.

Byron

Byron - wringing to and fro. How do we belie the time it takes – we can't. How do we nestle up to windings of fate? We can and must. There is an ease on the path, all we must do is find it. And there it is found. Never give in, that must is sure.

All the more reason to see a right. All the more reason to be the thought which never shirks. There is a fawning mass that has as itself the need of a thousand sailors, people who sail the sea, and know it to be free. Let us be, and see.

Byron – Are you with us, oh man of many tidings. There is a conch shell in which you can hear a thousand seas. Let us hear it then. Let us be the way of it. There is a new flower to smell, a new feeling to nourish. Have no rough call. We are there.

Hearing more of the same, we come for the white horse amongst us. And then, without refuge, we move again, to size up the distance between us. But what can this be? What can this be, that reminds us of the smile? We have never known else.

Byron – a serve of what is best. A puncture that holds in time. And here, where the world is suspended, there comes a mighty gurgle, one we can hear from all sides. Do not feel derision, the wettest part of the year is upon us. We will gather ourselves.

Gaining in stature, the method of our search comes to fruition. And then, without the hope to care, there transcends a day in the life of everybody that ever broached a net. Come now, do not be truly, deeply at ease – not yet. We must wait – yes.

Byron – do you tempt us with your trappings? Is this what we have come to expect? Fire and a little snow. We see your gauge, and have the residence to carpe your strongest eye. There is a nuance that we cannot find. Be still here, we must come.

Bleeding hearts, and implicit wings, there is a nice surprise behind all of us. What is its cause? Pure nothingness. What does it cement? The dreams of all of us. What is there left? But everything. And look, we see more than we ever have before.

Byron – You were quite adjacent to the wind when you lived. There is now a hollowed out shell in your honour. What have we found, but the range with various obsequies. There is more to this, of course – Your life lit up the stage.

Something sensory rounds out your life, but what have we to say? There is more in the ear-marking than we ever saw fit. Please come again, come again, for the ride of it. We are young at heart, and know the shallows to be with us.

Byron – looking back, do you see the hoops and renegade arms. Is this where the languishing of halves have their prey. I sense a new sense is terms of how far, and sub addition of the ready. There is now no turning of wings through the air. Yes.

Fishing for our lives, we come to the utmost of devilry. Here, we find something else of interest, something that entices as well as enchants. Have we the room, the room to say 'I do'? Come dancing in, there is nothing left to say. But we will say it.

Byron – are your bellows as long as the life? Do you come at speed, and then repent? Is there time to spend away? Do we whittle while we wait? The last of it gives leave of us. Do we tarry even longer, now that we are here? Come and see.

The castle by the sea, didn't match your abbey, Byron. Do you snatch at it even still? There is a circumventing that doesn't leave idleness astray. Come and see what you wish. There is adequate time for profession, and then we can see all we like.

Byron – is this the dire and the strange? Do we have the larder stocked? Is this all that is? From now until death? Sublime, intrepid, delightful. Is there a stock amongst it? Do we encourage more than taught? We are in the mode, you and I.

Verily, and harping. Have the riposte send us giggling. There is coming up, in the tempera-ment, a nice and pleasant motion. Do not be afraid, there comes nothing we could miss. Arch-ing a little bit at a time, and not seeing the aegis of it.

Byron – The sands of this glass are thoroughly yours. And without question, nothing can do what you did again. The arc of the regent comes in a pause, and then a stillness. We come for you, oh great one. We come and then are gone.

Heading off to the hills for another break. There are places, and then there are places. I am rectified, and then there is up, as there is down. Be the single light in an otherwise dark room. There can only be what is left. Yes, I will carry you through.

Byron - do you sense the unease? The unease at the bottom of things. There is more to say here, than meets the ear. There shimmers a nightly breeze, that handles itself in all that re-mains. And there, where the caustic wit of everyone comes. Stay.

Left to wander through night's transfiguring accomplishment, there is a sound that has no need to be at all. I am one to send the thoroughfare of desire back to where it came. And now, where we see ourselves again, we know just what is to come.

Byron – Planning the weep, we know what time the carriage comes in. It forever turns our way, forever bitten, forever dismayed. Come now, we must not linger longer than is conceivable. The tenacious and the proud.

What will become of us, the daylight few? The mass and the semblance. And then, when we are at the striving post, we see the tempers that overcome. And then, when the traffic of the promenade really reaches a crescendo, nothing, nothing that quits.

Byron – All most all of this is at the benchmark. Almost all of this sees the mist. Why the mist? Beautiful, but obfuscating. Blissful, but difficult. Hard to see through, but not hard. There is a life here, one that is not of this world. Come, never renege.

Having more than what it is worth. Being a start, in a simple world. Hanging on, despite the dawn. Hanging on, despite the known in things. We prove liberal in the sheen and bark of it. There is something more to it than we can say.

Byron – needing acclaim, the boisterous in the line says I can go. And then, heaving with half breaths, there is a cataclysmic reluctance to assail us. What is there now, I hear you say? What is there now? I come for acceptances, and work out aloud.

Commiserating, and knowing no time. There is this, and this alone. A fabric that entails no wandering. A sense of life itself. A sense that the roundness of this entreaty will come full cir-cle. And then, the watch word that sings itself to sleep.

Byron – do you see the way? Is this how you play? And then, a nature to it all, one that shy's away from the verdure of the night. There are lesson's to be learned here. But who shall learn them? There are plays on plays, but who keeps word.

Gaining in momentum, there is now a solemnity that follows, and follows in deep solitude. And here, we venture forth, venture into the rallying point of a number of gravesides. We will point this way and that. And then, before long, life.

Byron – containing all measurement. Containing all forgiving. There is a chance to wander into the footfalls of tomorrow This is something special, but we will not find it easier than sand to come here. This must we must march on our own.

Having to do something inside and out, and then, when the porcelain is all done, there comes a sound of increasing lassitude. And then, without the need to comply with the silence, there comes a grit that takes us onto the next town.

Byron – There is a light sort of feeling, that lingers as it does on the doors of an ancient forest. And then, when the light is brought from the solstice, there is new need to rush out of doors, and have as our sun, the noise.

Foremost in our minds are the wounds we shed. Here, where the most ardent of passions are derived from the earth, there is something more, something that savours the day, and gives light to willing. Have the time at your disposal.

Byron – there is in your lap, a thing that cannot be named, but which has all the trappings of fate. Come and see the mirror, before your tea boils over. It is more like the treasure we find in search of the temperance we seek – stay strong.

Throwing forward everything that can be, there is something that cannot be seen. And here, where the noise of engine's past, clicks up into the wheel again, there let's be the semblance of the night. Come and see, there is something new here.

Byron - you described your dog, Botswain, upon his passing, as having 'beauty without vanity, strength without insolence' You loved animals, this is true. And let the passage of time herald in something more, and something more still.

Couching up to the centre of things, like tomorrow was just a dream. There is more like the density that we breathe, and the solitude we harbour. Let not one split the other. Let all that will be, be. There can only be the life of it, still.

Byron – are you the person we think you are? Are you the moisture in the air, that sometimes frightens and bites? There is a new thing here that agrees when it fastens, and has as no questions when it leaves. No questions? Yes, No questions.

Holding to the state of things with nothing more that sweaty hands, there is more than enough to slide off the map. And here where the danger has not past, the single most poignant thing is said, and that let go of. Mast, it is true.

Byron

Byron - do you live? And not in decay? Is this what we feel for you, in the trance, in the night? Is the time just right, right in stature, and in negligence? I have never seen this before. This in lounge. And when we find our way out of the sky – then.

Lost in the seething of it, there comes a new type of adventure. One in which the cowards of the daylight do not sense the nuances of the daylight hours. And now, with the feeling of tempestuous irreverence, something to hold on to.

Byron - Nestled in close, there is a feeling like we never were. And in this time, and in this de-livered beauty, there comes a lost tangent, that knows no other way. And here, where the cost knows nothing, the belligerence of time sends for another day.

What is the new type of salience that covers our feet? What is this thing we seek? Is it in the meantime that the playing of scoundrel's love is like the hardship of desire? We are left to find our place in amongst it. We will sing again.

Byron – have you had your fill? Your apogee to the four walls? And then the disarray to spark a nation? There are times to see things aright, and times to see things wrong. And then, as if we had not seen anything worth seeing – life.

Catching nothing of value, and nothing of the scent. There is a likeminded harrowing, that blends with the times, or not at all. We all contain what we need, and as the present is like a free-for-all, there comes a happenstance that hears nothing more.

Byron – Having the courage, but not having the clothes. Or having both. We see, in the furthest places, what it is that keeps us underwhelmed. And then see, what we need to be. Come and sense what it takes, an overwhelming question?

Leasing on life, we have foretold the sky his most ardent passion. And then, when we least expect, a co-mingling with the sea, that has as its waist everything that we could ever dream. Be a water down, that lingers but does not stay. Let us focus.

Byron – are you the one to sail the seas of your native England, and have as its calling the last stencil to remedy. We are coming to rest here – but we have much to go. And when we are through, we are through. What cannot be contained is in here.

And then, when the fashion of the day is up, we raise ourselves even higher. And without a care, we fall unto our need that treasures in silk. What is the upward drift of the scaling we are doing? Does it get in the way, or does in press hard upon?

Byron – the woods are clear of any compulsion to jump or laugh. But that is what we thought in the meantime. What is that which we felt, can only be what is encompassed in the dawn. Never wandering, always firm. Come quick.

The tide has nothing to say, as the land beach curtails the side-long cradle. Be a starfish in a world of excitement. There is one thing that cannot be loved here, and that is us. We are cer-tain about one thing; the words are with us.

Byron – calculated to fall, you rise. And in this motion, you set the incumbency adrift, and feelings and commiserations, around you. I hope that the window for the soul is like things that have never been ridden. We love that which is a naming.

Byron

Hallowed and a test of the times, we cease to wander what life is, and just simply live it. And then, when the dire and the straight come for the trouncing A feather like the one we saw yes-terday. Static in the air it seemed. We will find ourselves again.

Byron – come forward and see things anew. Come in the witching hour, and then disappear. The time which is spent can never be recast. And then, the marvel of everything comes, in great shades of delight. Do not linger – to linger is to last.

Forward to the tune of the last hurrah, and then back again to where we are. The stampede in the invective comes in straight, and then out again. The greater more that dreams play in our lives, is like the shambolic and the rouse, all in one.

Byron – What we thought was the majesty of the realm, is nothing other than the fairy hill that plays upon the night of mist. What have we found, but the light on tender hooks? What have we believed, but the round, and the sill? Come now.

Gaining grace from each dance, we more up in register each passing day. And then, when the ever-reaching fairy house never falls, the didactic and the strange wallow in the same mud, there is a considerable disease amongst things.

Byron – letting never ending turquoise reach your bed. Letting the fact of what is never reach your ears. The circumstances we find ourselves in never diminish in size, always getting larger. And then, without aplomb, things requite.

The salience of the dare gives a new found voice to old acquaintances. And then, when the time is amongst us, the things we do to stave off the night and the trouble of the vociferous. I am one never to wander, never to enjoy the journey.

Byron – do you see yourself in steeds of fire, steeds of desire? And then when the daylight never quite illuminates, there is a sense, that has long since gone – a sense that the things you find are for the fellow travellers.

The tenderest part of the day is here. And when we see things in their most majestic aspect, we never forget. And then the well-spring of lie's river takes hold, nothing can be seen other-wise. But what of what is next? Can we even tell?

Byron – in the mean-time, we sing a soulful tune, and have the rest come to rest. There is next to us, a fathoming shore, that brings as its greatness, the hollowed-up meeting of two lonely hearts. But what do we say, when things stay awry?

Much in line with what comes next, the simplicity of the water knows no rest. And here, where the sunlight never perishes, the light of aeons flares in untold ways. What comes, colours a nation. Neither this nor that; but this.

Byron – messing with the guard duty, I see your love implode on shores of remembering, shores of belief – belief in things untold. What do we say, when things loan themselves to the wind, never wanting to sense the arrow straight?

Coaxing out the errand, before it has had a chance to be done. And then, when we see the rightful passage, there exhumes more than enough steam to complete the journey. Hoping something of the sound of it comes around. Playful and astute.

Byron – a listless abounding that gives with it the hope of far-flung residencies. There is now said for lane that has in time the much-abused tenacity. Come forth, and see the longing we all new we had. Longing for all that is best.

Is the twist what we have? Is this the sound of a at last found island? There is now something in the right place, and the right time. And there, where the stars shine in placid union. There is enough to scold the dawn.

Byron - are you in the way of it? Do you speak with hands, and with tongue? Does the libretto fit the scene - poverty and a wisp of adventure? Do we harp on as yesterday, today, and to-morrow? Come now for the complexity of sun dancing.

Voicing our concern, the little and the march have not had their say. And then, without the need to fashion a raft that will take us there, there is a need to feed the animals in your me-nagerie. Come now do not fix a screw, it will settle in time.

Byron – do you harvest the sense we have to march, march at full speed? There is a sem-blance of forgiveness in all that you say. And here, where the words hold full sway, they are listening for the right hub, to nestle in like an eagle, and then away.

Votive and insouciant, and never both at the same time. There is a sense we have known that languishes as we speak, it loves as it gathers, and trumps as it re-invigorates. The seeds of this parsimony needs no explanation.

Byron – Speaking through the room, we dust off our summer jackets and know there to be room. And now, where we come from is not at risk, but what we thought was a stallion is but a show, there comes a little bit showman in all of us, every bit.

Vanquished, but alive, the drive is continued, and survives. What the mirror asks, can not help us. We laugh in mixed volume contagion, and a sense, what the market is for. We have not left you yet, we beings of the night. We will come again.

Byron – aforementioned only in the Greek. And then only with a scolding. Belittle the flame not, it is for him we speak, and for him we come. There is a time to chance, and one to remain settled. And here we see both, if that be possible.

Gathering ourselves for the pleasure of it, we miss the turn that paled red. And here, where the tropes are in the wind, our syncopated composure does not miss the whole for a second. And then, intrigued, a new way to be. What is left?

Byron – a missive in the sea. Is it your hand writing? Is it the coast you miss? I can only say that the reflexes are good, and the health of the organism rings true. Do not say anything less doctor. That is right, health is with the missive.

Constant exposure to the elements, that soon belittle what they defy. Catching the rainbow is soon our repartee, but we will not lose it, not for anything, nor anyone. Fencing off the door-way, to get a sturdier vantage. We will come.

Byron – the nearness of the thing. Its contiguity. I feather you not. There is nothing here to feather. And that is a plot in itself. Something at speed. Something we are handy to divine, and wish the last of it on strings of aching leather.

Do you come again, my pet? Is this where there is outlandish behaviour? I am one to sense a comment – let it come. What will we say, when we have arrived? Will be too overcome to the melting of butter, that we lose our composure.

Byron – is this your run? Come and see. Everyone has a run in them. Look at mine, for in-stance. And what about that of the loneliness or the aplomb. Can you see it my Byron? There is a feather to be struck, struck into gold. Yes, and again.

A gushing of everything so sweet. Is this what we say, when saying is hirsute. A never where care, that is homely, and unobtrusive. Do we stand in something of the way, is the local and the bastion reneging, do you think for much of the time?

Byron – seeing into things, never capturing a moment. Always being at the vanguard of fate. What is left, is never wanting. And there, where we come in terms with the vicarious there belittles no drum. What have we left? The saving grace.

Bewildered, but not betrayed. There is life in us still. And then, where the mighty have a hold on us, we will sing, replete with careless wonder. Is this what we seek, in the utmost holding of any hand. The utmost believing in the nature of the world.

Byron – come, do not bind, do not shackle yourself to the surface of it. There is much to see, and much to do. Come now, we are here to shake things, shake things out. What have we to hear, but all that is? What are we to see – but all that can be seen?

Never mind the rub, that sand between our toes is enough. And there, where the dice are thrown in absentia, there minds a mighty sublimation, that comes to give way to all things. Never finding things easy, we fight for all that is left.

Byron – a likeminded shrill sound. There is something we come for again and again. And that is you, air, and not drowning out, we see, just as before. The missive of yours I have found in the wake of the ship calls wonders. And then.

A modesty that has as its yoke the temporality of the sky itself. What is this we find, here, amongst it all, we find love, and a calling card, and never a moments rest. There is something that saves us from ourselves, so let us see.

Byron – A majesty that awaits confirmation. This is what we see, and what we hear – I know of no other way than this. The home we find is lascivious. The home we find is simply what awaits. Never shying away. Never beating a retreat. Never.

A riotous feeling that has the sense to wander. Almost new, there comes a time to blunder. And here where we beckon a token asunder, there remains a truth to all of this. A truth that never starts in fits and spurts. Come now, we must go.

Byron – There is an act most gracious, most in line with the heart and all it entails. What does your mother say to you at your first broken heart? What did she council? What spirit did she induce? The law is there, my friend. The law of the world.

Byron

Coming closer to the sanctioning of winter heartbeats. There is now a light sighted being, who comes in the station, to blister past, and through. What is it that he does? He gathers pace, and knows how to swim, and knows to write.

Byron – do you hear the call, the call to dream? Do you wander in inches, and not miles, as we all do? Do you swim in miles, and not inches? Is that where we have found our water, despite the art of spring. There is now an architecture to form.

Clashing and guarding – the twin masts of the day. And here, where, the silence lives, there a place, that hears our cries for what they are - new needs to help. And then, an awkward awry, that stampedes through the bookshop.

Byron – On your reconnaissance through the world, what did we see that gave your pleasure? What did you see that put you of a beat? What did you see, that simply needed to be seen? Rocks and mortar's ash. Come now, we are there.

Not being one to sport a festive bravado, there is one who blinks in times of unease, and times of reticence. Come to me now, we must away. Can we come to help at all? I hope so. And then the renting of the fibres of life. Come now, we are there.

Byron – having a laugh with the rest of us. Feeling full of life, and not stranded on that island in the sun. There is living, and there is living. Utmost, and serene. Clearing, and then undoing. What is this mist that envelopes us?

Having the sense to continue, despite the link to a future that has the sails on the test of it. The majesty of the wind will get us there. And then, with the patience of a window pane, that no one can pull up, or down. See it through, we will come.

Byron – like a wig in the night. Like a treasure that burns luminosity. There are things that have as their release all the stars in the sky, and then more. Do not renege, or see yourself as through. There comes testimony from high places.

Lost in the middle of it. Lost without the need to see. I have a motion to give all of you. It mat-ters not what the harbinger will say, and say again. We have the left to its right, the up to its down. We have what is fruitful, and what is laden.

Byron – a surge in the middle of it should do the trick. And here, where the feather does only float, there winds a lonely trail, in amongst the most open plain that has yet to be conceived. Come now, sense is away.

Lasting, and not committing. Being challenged, and not cursing. The things we thought were awe-full are only the things which keep us going. Do not sing for cover, the plentiful and the wise encounter this domain. They will win.

Byron – offshoots of the sublime that have as their stasis a new sort of thing. Committed to the cause, one day at a day, being a little laden with overarching, we see things as they are, not as they were. Let us in, and through, and beyond.

Listening in, feeling tender, being lopsided, but still not falling over. There is a chance in amongst it that will only be true for a certain time. There can only be the sense we have, even in the tide of it. There can only be this, and this only.

Byron – we are moving forward, and up, and beyond. Do not belittle the time spent, it is some-thing other. There is now a time to recuperate, and a time for setting forth. Do not choose veri-ly, but against the grain. More can be said.

Everything moves forwards. Everything that is moving backwards, is in actual fact moving for-wards. Everything that is moving up, is moving forward. These words stem from the knowledge of things. And there, behind these words, is poetry.

Byron – harvesting the grain, we see the sense of the stars, and have our needs re-arranged to accommodate them. The liking of the kings, we sense once more the wind that does not hiss. And then when we hear that sound most heard…

Foreign to us, the land lies low in our sights. There is a sort of gnashing of teeth that occurs here, and knows that the way through is another time around the corner. What we have found is that the moisture of the sky will never be enough.

Byron – A force that has no power. A nestling that has no wrath. Foraging in and amongst it. A joy that has the portent of it. Something small, that turns big. There is life through and through. The marks that are left are not deep, nor long.

A forest with no trees. A landing, that has its base the newness of the sanguine heart. The mess we have left is not one to clean easily, but we shall, out of respect of those journeymen that rumble a keepsake, especially on par with us.

Byron – seething in the mist, we come with apron on, and see ourselves in dawn coloured attire. And then, without the need to retreat, there comes a full-blown residue, one that wreaks of the merriment of delight. Come, let us go.

Finishing off the moisture from the troupe, will, with time to spare, come in to considerable aplomb. Is there a need now, to give the light away, as so much flotsam, and then reaching further, further than ever before?

Byron – leaning upright, the mews no longer say what is supposed to be said. And then, a question for you Byron – do you reach for the quill that got you there, the one that started your journey? Or do you reach from you last one in the journey?

Have you listened to anything at all? Is this the way to proceed, through alleys and side-glimpsed hopes. There is more like the fashioning of hues, that has as a round-a-about, the newness of times coming again. Remember this, if you must.

Byron – Are you laden with fruit? Do your clothes have themselves a way with them? Do you arc on angles that are straight? Is this the way to be short with the crowd? I know of no other way. Simplify the passage of time, and we will see.

Much is said about your life, much that is never short of finding. There is here, a time-piece that has as its derivative the journey of the square. We catch under the night sheet, and then above the mantle, and all that is left is for good.

Byron – are you one to smile at the calling of the day – of the day-break and of its motion. There is like a wood in the wind, if that makes sense. There is now a temperance that is interminable, that harks back, to all that is.

Eloping to the sound of the bushels, there remains an autumn we can trace. And there is the wind of it, there consists a tethering of this to that, of here to there. Lock and unlock, the party of troubadours knows only one way – through.

Byron – are you there, my friend? Are you one to sense the realms around, and see to it we find ourselves nothing but the agile and the cane. Despite ourselves, there is a truce to be made, a truce that is left to skies bell, and the rest.

Feeling like the sense we all have that life is made for adventure, and life is made for the one thing we all miss, and that is trust. The further we go, the further we seek. The further we seek, the further our eyes are made clear.

Byron – having a fresh start, and being ready to continue. There is more than the comingling of stars that can stop us. The westerly direction of all things is in repose to a mighty thump. And the sound it makes is more than we can transcribe.

All the more reason to stay, to stay to that more meandering place. We find our self with air to take us there, takes us there, and more. What is left is nothing more than the sense we believe in, the sense to have a dash at it. Yes, let us go.

Byron – whispering under sycamores, whispering through the forest, and through the trees. There is a licentiousness that we can stop, but choose not to. Can we figure things out in the time it takes to randomly move the earth?

Racing to the line of the soul, there is more than we can say, or ever really feel. Come and see things afresh, this thing that knows no things. And then the falling of rain, that comes in cascades, rumbling down from the sky. We will find a way.

Byron – has your race been run? Is this the utmost you can do? I sense a feeling in the water of the now, a feeling I have not heard from time immemorial. What is this thing of which we write? Can it be in the now – let's look, and see.

Visions of the visionary. There is a happening that deifies both. But in defying, leaves us re-splendent. Come now the pall is upon us, and upon us still. There wanders all the waters ever known. There wanders all the waters ever known – and then a dash.

Byron - is this what we have in store – in store for the winter months. There comes a timing that is replete in the lodge of it. Do not prescribe a remedy, we need none. And here where the laughter twitches and turns, there can come a singular.

Modest in trait, the oxymoron delegates all responsibility. And here, where the distance of this space to another is more like the trembling of an all-out predilection, there comes a noisy ves-tige, that holds only the sound in check.

Byron – conscious of the need to be in tune with the rest. There is no time for the partiality of the sun to the stars. And then, with much writing in the in-between time, we come aghast, and blow sweet bubbles through and through – we must.

Harbouring the distance like never before. Giving, instead of its fortitude. And then like the way we hold things here. The way we stay to vie for the rest. In the middle of an adventure of organic magnitude, we see ourselves through.

Byron – are you lost, lost to time itself? I can see your passage in winters day light, and here, where we see things aright once again, the danger is past, and the falling of midnight enve-lopes all that is. Come what do you say? We will see.

 Yes, and then the playing ceased - the playing ceased. What we found in the middle of the lane is something that should not be lauded. What was in the lane, is something to be lauded. Come and see the truth of it, settling down.

Byron – letting the silence drain away. Letting the nicety of it all drown us. Drown us in seas of remorse, for not doing the dusty idleness. What has become of the horizon? We do not know. What has become of the land? We do not know.

Seraphim wax that closes in on time. Witnessing as the long-lost footfalls join in to take on time, and keep winning, and keep fighting, keep punching, keep round, that type of thing. There is a flagstaff that we can keep, keep to let us in the door of life.

Byron – a message in the sun dance, a dance that doesn't swing. And here, where the mois-ture is long drawn, the template for the daylight runs strong. And then, in the subtlety of the rain, something of great hue emerges. Never before seen.

Witnessing the twilight, as if it was a fact. Giving all the major tracts, something to lie on. And here, where there is a sound for every voice, and town for every plateau, something cautious and implacable, something new, that was once old.

Byron - Whispering on a breeze, a life that bites back. And then, when the cares of a millennia stay firm, and now, the tallest sense of wellbeing is ensnared, we will find a way. The canary and the lizard launch forth, to tell of things unseen, unknown.

Forthwith, and for-to-come. Being busy, and having the night without a sense to believe. A needing that is caught in the fence, and something that wanders before we leave. What is there here but memories and ghosts. We will not surrender.

Byron – are you the one to sleep in amongst it? No, of course you are not. Are you the one to sense the folly of our ways? I think you could be. The testimony to the arbour of the vision of things comes in round-a-bouts and springs. We will hear.

There are even more than the things we thought were asleep, even in amongst it. Dishes to the departed, glasses raised, nobility in check, who have found the way through. There can only be one way, one way despite the rest. We will see.

Byron – caught in amongst the thistle, there is time to raise a ruckus, and find the way home once again. Listening now, we send the rendering of urban mass unto the faith of the once and only king. What do we fight for, in front of us?

Letting go of the sky, that has carried us so far. We hear ourselves in motions of nuances, that swing and have soul, and have the need to drive home the stance we all took. The sense of it is bespoken in the wind, that rises as it dilates.

Byron – The belittling of the nobody arches, is enough to send the cautionary out to dry one thousand times to come. And then then the shifting of the motion beginnings, there is a chal-lenge of a different hue to be overcome. We will fight, and fight.

Byron

Being along-side of the castle wall, the moss, which, turns an ancient direction, in more than one tide, has as its sustenance the wheels of an auburn cart. Just send us there, to the bed-rock, and the folly. Just send us there, wrinkle and prayed.

Byron – a sense we have that the stars are never enough to protect us. That the sky cannot do the same, and here, where the juice of life has the fur to see again, the limestone jar has the safety just to speak. We will find away. We will find away.

Economising to the fruit of it. Lying beside the sand, and seeing the sea. What we thought could not be contained. What we knew was purely pleasant. The sanction of the work of art. There is no greater expression in the armoury. Let us continue.

Byron – you know how to tread. You know how the music goes. Even your diatribe against the new Waltz, I sure, meant much to you. And then, inscribed in nature, there remains the hollow, the hollowed-out wood. Enough, let us go.

Closing the shores of indemnity, we race once again to that place in the inner sanctum, that shores are wedded to, and needs are met. Catching nothing of the meaning of it, we silence the dawn, with bouts of lingual ferocity.

Byron – do you clasp all that is. Do you send the middle of it, the middle of it, to the outer edge? There is now a thing that binds, and binds in times of structure and remorse. The thing we see, is over the high and over dale. Yes, not missing.

Completing the fire act, for all and sundry, and being the way we doing things here. The once and open delight, that only knows one way. There is a feeling that knows no vice. That feeling is once and only once, unless there is more to say.

Byron – are you awake? Do you seethe in amongst it, to know it, to feel it? Is that what we say is biting the humdrum out of us? There can be now more. There can be no more. And then witnessing the forge, come, and flashes of steel.

Brining our barge out of the water for repairs. There is something ancient about this ritual. Something to see us through. It is a ritual that has as it keeps the water of every harbour that has ever know a drenching. Come now, we must away.

Byron – listening to the forest, I see you – I see you, Byron. Do you play in the forest as woodsman on a break? Do you see what is left of us still? Do you tense onto the hills, unto the valleys? Is this where we have come to? We shall see.

Bending, and breaking, reaching, and bleeding. There is ferocity of insight that does not belittle the place it was born. The tenderness of the worn-out soul knows no boundaries, more than is foretold. There comes a tension that is released.

Byron – foregoing, and foretelling, there is never more than what can be accomplished. Do you see the grave for what it is? A piece of sand amongst the rubble. Always respected, never with time, and never with spark. Come, tomorrow.

The bottles of festive intransigence, have come full circle, and have let their missive come to the tempest of things. The larger the shinning, the larger the happenstance, the larger the ex-planation. We will see the time it takes.

Byron

Byron – are you the one to see deeply into things? Do your wings fly vertically, and your treasured leap, does that come down with you now? I have a thought, which is for you Byron. Do you trudge on bearings, bearings that surely well get you there!

Brittle, and like ice. Brittle, and like the sea in winter, which nothing can break. The test in the sea shore, where it comes too little and too late. The immensity of which we speak, is nothing other than the baby breath at first hour. And here we tremble.

Byron – messages from the abyss. I write to today, not in fear, but in heart felt memory, that is like a new fledgling through the mist. We come, as much as in love as in anything else, and here we know we will be again.

Many messages to come. Many ways to be safe. Many delights in store. Many fathomless seas to measure. What more could we hope for, what more could we see? The further we plumb the depths, the higher we rise for the heights.

Byron - Coming close to the edge of things, we never think of being outclassed. And here, where the noise is at its peak, we find ourself anew. And here we are then, dismantled, but on time. We come for you, next, and all the night unblemished.

There is a place here, and a feeling, that has never been evoked. They say things arrive in threes, but what is that but the engine of our concern. It spicks and spurts, and gets underway. And then without care of anything whatsoever!

Byron – coming in despite the word of mouth, much that has gone on, will go on. There is a sky filled with gems, such that they love the way they are mended. The times about this sky, are beauty personified. A red mist appears, and then...

Lingering for hours at a time, the dispelled and erased headpiece, gathers the way in some-how new and unheard-of types of being. We are new when it comes to this. But in the mael-strom, a sense we have that things will right themselves.

Byron – rising ourselves up, we cling to the very fibres of what comes next. And here, where we galvanise ourselves for the journey, we sense again that the mission ahead is like an anathema not to be looked upon lightly. Here are go then!

Forcing the part in the sea, we have found our way, and the journey seems better. We have what is lost, and what is found, and what can never be upright to the stars. Come for the feel-ing of hardship, and know the closeness of the steady race.

Byron – are your remorses as thick as the ground below? Do you sense the coming of an age, an age that defies no logic, nor transverses any field? There are ancient manuscripts to pe-ruse. To see the stamp of yore, you gather things again.

High, and away, we see the ground sink, and then explode upward, into the air. Do not right the ship, there is too much at stake. And here, where we own the beaches upon which we stand, there is something like forever revealed.

Byron – a fine marksman you were, and good at showing of your skill. But what of the taint of not being one to settle yourself before a dozen good men, who had not heard of you, nor read your works? We hear their call, and listen to their orders.

Byron

Fathom the abyss, and like it never was. There is never a saint nearby, when you need one, nor closer when you don't. The mistress of the land upon which we walk, never raises a canter when we say oh, missy, come to play overtures.

Byron – singing that sultry song, the has no feeling in it, nor life to settle into. Are we yet a hinderance, are we yet a tune on the lips of very sailor that has swept the sea? There is a constant refrain, that believes in nothing expect the wind, and the daylight.

Nestled in closely, the time it takes to be what we were, is now, and not then, is here but not when. There comes a travelling, as there comes a cake to eat by the side of the road. And here where the sands of tide duly meander, there is life that nestles.

Byron – coming in quickly, its silhouette knows no stopping, nor no round-a-bout speed. And then, a life, one in amongst it. There is time to wind the bell, to new tensions. What comes next? We will only know when we are there.

Reaching out to the feather – it knows no bounds. And here, where the warbling of tenor birds reaches the night, there is much to see, and much to do. I have found a way through the deserted streets, and into the presence of much more.

Byron – is that which we saw, is that which the hour also saw? Can we march into one, and march out of time? Is this what the both of us knew to be true. Come now, we are enlivened, in speech as in tears. There is something more here.

Looking back, having the span to handle the way. We look for the lead, and then we announce ourselves – once, twice, three times – and then through, and up and beyond. We can never be that fjord to rustle up things. We are there to be.

Byron – an annoying side-post, that gathers no likely-hood, until to the fashion of the day re-news. Do not fall for the keepsakes, they are here to hinder. Verily they specify the new and the old. More signposts, than what alleviates. Come, we are there.

Never in one go, never in the mists of it does it come. There are messages in the sand, sand that heats as it rivals March. Heats as it has no heat to bare. Have some fruit, and do not settle for the rotunda, it is here that we see our course.

Byron – there are things amongst it, my Byron. There are things that ladle only spirit, and things that only have heart. There is use, and nonsense, in the way of it. Come close to us, there is a pent-up rage that has nothing to spill. Yes, again

Coping with the twilight, there are many things we wish to see. How many are the tailors in this part of the world? How many are the lost and the found, we can always give some assistance. Come for it all, never again.

Byron – Run with the trees – do as you please. And then (hiccup), and then (burp) and then, just have your way. We find time to do what we want. We find the time to say nothing out of character. Nothing duly noted, nothing at all.

Giving the rangers a second glance, saying what is out of respect. Distances that hear you chuckle. What we once loved, but no longer have the stomach for. What we have found to be a truth in the making. Saying to ourselves, yes we should.

Byron – the role of the steam engine, chuttering down the track. Feeling the way of it, never looking back. Cold, and smart, and in the truest sense, through. Where we never look. And yes, a new a lightning strike. A strike that comes back in halves.

We could never be the one to shy away from a fight. There is little by little no body left. Nobody left to conquer. Nobody left to foil the show. Do not linger in the shadows, there will be time to have fun again.

Byron – people have found the raining down of the music of the moon a source of pleasure, what is in it for the rest of us? We soothe our bonds, and have as cheerful sway, the long re-turning envelope that guards, as long as it sleeps.

Holding sway, or holding court, or doing both, we come again to show ourselves the way of it. And then when the singing never ceases, a moisture in the air. Come now, there is nothing remiss, there is only solid nomenclature, and then a way forward.

Byron – what is the sound it makes? What is the rinsing of the tongues for? There is only a semblance of the discompose of an all-day response. Come, do not be loud, do not be the things that keep us there. There is more to say, and more to do.

Never missing in scale, the worst of it lags. And here, where we purchase the totems in action, there is a remorse for the rest of it. Coming close to the heart of things, there is a majesty we just don't see. But here, where we come, there are flowers!

Byron – have the position at the ready. We know what we are in for! Come like a dancer in the dark – dancing all the while. I come for an appraisal of things to come. But here, where the future is in untold sanctity, the guise often assumes fine.

Hiding in the mist, there resides a chance to linger in untold ways, and untold days. We are here with you, and your fruit laden basket. There is a temptation to eat, but we must not. Just looking fills the soul. And here, a rapacious endeavour.

Byron – lending ourselves to the journey – we come full circle, and know the start to be the end, and the end to be the start. What is more, the length of the journey, is in full measure. What do we find for ourselves – nothing that can be sanctioned.

Full, and in extremis, the land we have met, comes with us to the estuary, and then beyond, into the sea. What is this we seek, from all the harbours to the now? From everything that ris-es, to everything that falls. To the teeth of it, and through.

Byron – are you well? Have you survived this time? I think, at a guess, yes, you have. And now, all there is to be done is land a rope through the bitterness. And see the function of the things we share. The things we share, and catch upon.

We are there, to both of us – thanks to the fool who has nothing but wisdom and thanks to the libretto that knows itself to be one after the other. There are things we cannot cross here, things we must not seal with any kiss, or any life-force.

Byron

Byron – how far have you been? How far have you to go? There are challenges here that want their want in gold. Challengers here, that desire all that can be desired. And then, without the slightest incentive, a new task to beckon old fights.

Furthering the likeness to the dimensions, we see ourselves in folds of whims and gold. The first taste we had, was never one to shy away from. The first taste we had, was a much-needed respite – respite from the hardships of the journey.

Byron – why did your writing always convince the tribe, and never the merriment of others? You fought for the way of it – a new way, and a new coaxing of winter warmth. Do not be bra-zen here, there is time for the wandering of souls.

Fixity like nothing else. Fixity in the realms of numbers and letters, numbers and letters, you have no heart for the sky of it. But that is okay, the jumpers are for play, and jackets are for ac-tion. Can you polish the way we walk, for the life of it?

Byron – does the fish swim for you, or against you? So the weathering of ancient fireflies see us come again to the shore, to the shore of all that is. We are more concerned now that you have left, than ever before. That is okay, we have a way.

Holding up in the sand, that has as the hounded a new found release. Come now, and sense the toil, sense the toil of more than a hollow will be sure of. There is now a lasting fitting, that belittles the stark reminders of the day. Come, and be one.

Byron – are you cleverer by halves, and cleverer than some? I have now the sense of it, and reiterate my concern. Come for the fairground, stay for the days of it, and the months and the years. Stay for the much need fare, that stays then some.

Forming a stage, upon which shall sit all of them, every single one of them. All those that cast a brick unto the raining of the light. All those who never fashioned a rapidity with the stars, and had what was good in the meantime. Come now, we must away.

Byron – linking arms, and being afresh. Doing what we must, to still all hearts. Being the sort of person who will guide to the last. There is now a sort of harping that has as its base the threads of time itself. And there we are, through.

Gaining strength from within. Gaining in momentum, from without. There are things we have never seen before, never seen, never felt, never wandered, never coalesced. Be true to us, guides of yore, yours is an important role.

Byron – helping us, help ourselves – and here a truism. One that knows the length of the de-parture. I have found in this lot many turns of phrase, but one that must be remembered, is this – always run for cover when it is raining!

Galvanising, and throwing an ebb, the lowest one at that. Being ready, but ready for what? Being inside all the while, and not seeing the birches. Come and see something more from us. Come and be the withering, as you are the bowl.

Byron – having to land from your perch, quickly. Having to saddle your horse in a hurry. See, there is no further passage, passage in time for the up-hill haul. The times we had are gone but not elongated. Come for the well, it is us.

Byron

The very nature of these things is pursuant on the district, and here we come for the home we never knew. Have the steel to wither what is more, and not incredulous. Be the lasting of fences and the trenching of houses – we will be, and never be less.

Byron - hugged, and then believed. The flounce is one of confidence – and seems carefree. There is much we must say. Even more we must do. Let us hurry back, to that time immemori-al, the misty climb, the edge of things.

Coming like a horse through the narrows, wisping like we never gave a care. And here, let us see it. We have known many things, this horse and I, and now we have a simplicity at our stride, something to tail away the years.

Byron – are you fit to ride, my man? Is this the direction we should go? To double the bill, there is a rain stone in the harvest, we come from here to there, and back again. This time we will proceed, and then follow ourselves a burrow.

A languishing in the middle of it – we knew what would come. But that is not what we see now that we are there. We see things in that peculiar strain of time that is the west wind and the fathoming of the rind. Come to us, much needed souls. Come.

Byron – listening as tailor might, while being at his own domain. There are feelings at the crossing of borders, something that we might express, thus – never before, never again, only loving for a second, and then carrying on through.

Blemish, and recoil, calling for the sense of it, calling for the right way to go. Having the turn of speed to go with it. Being missed, and then coming through. What did we say at the end of it – gosh, we remember that.

Byron – the harlequin man at arms. What did fate have in store for you? You remember, I think – come now fully and absolutely, you are one to dabble only in the important. Do you say with assurance, let them all come?

The testament to the ground, the all falling inward, in the trance of it. Something blows through main sail giving movement. Lending time – seeing all, having the mischief to survive. Having that which is haunting, but not denied.

Byron – crossing off the fire with three modes to one. And now, we can persist, and in the mightiest blow, we sense the fire back in the most desperate of situations. And now, yes, there is more to do. More to say, more to lay to rest.

Saying a ritual goodbye, we move through the angles for a further look. There is something we cannot believe, except for the utter proximity of it. There is a moisture in the air, but how do I feel it – because it never leaves.

Byron – sluggish at heart, those raffish looks take you to where you want to go. The constant state of disrepair, a constant need of the whole – there is nothing left. What is there here but the chosen well that comes to be in each and everyone of us.

The vision we all see is that of Byron in his last days. But what of the days before his epic de-parture? Equally at odds with the mundane. But now we should not abandon a man so fit to be the ruler of a wide kingdom.

Byron

Byron - blistering forth, having the need and the desire to feel every inch of his life. Every iota. Every considerable flame. Does the mist lie here – it does -how does it show itself, through the withering that can never come.

Mismatching the way we walk. Misinterpreting so much. Being of a mind to say, yes, we can march on. Does the season run full measure here – I am sorry, I must ask, are you the shep-pard? This much, and more is clear.

Byron – swinging down from the world, to reach that semblance that can only be termed poet-ry. And here, where, the sounds of the ages come in spiralling formations, there is a sound that the ages cannot curtail. Let us listen.

An art gallery newly refurbished, holds your words on its walls for future generations. And here, yes here, the nightly scrawl finds windows in silk, and dandelions in-between things. What have we sought, by the time of day? What have we sought?

Byron – coughing and spluttering, never knowing what will come next. There are times in amongst it when we don't know how we will get through, but that is okay, we have not lost our senses. What is this, I hear you cry? What is this?

Farming right out to the edge of things – we stop for a deeper look, a deeper look at the depth of things. And then, without so much as a cry or a whimper, we see what we want to see, and that is life, yes, life. Fashioning the height of things.

Byron – And what has all this given us? What has all this given us, except that lonely road, that has never been travelled before? The standing we do out of the rain, is all that we can do. All that is available to us is something we never thought possible.

Festooned in the right fashion, of the right height. And here, we gauge the life we have left in turns of speed that lack no lustre, nor share no flight of bids above. An epicentre for what is to come next. Have your stoic turn of phrase. It will come.

Byron – Never once staying neutral, but always on the pitch. What has the land, as the ocean beats the shore? Come now, we must only have as the tangent all the wool we need. There is something more than this – we will see.

That distant arc. It levels all things, and has as its height the chambers of disregard. Come forward now, the limp we have is not ours to curtail. There is more in times of trouble than this. What have we found, but everything?

Byron – holding on, hanging on, holding a book to shield us from the day. This is all we can do. But what do we say, when things get awkward? What do we feel when others are nearby? There is now a solemn acceptance – one that drives.

Forming a gap in amongst our fellows, so that we can see them. And here, ramshackle and tutored, there is a new sense to old wounds. I have not seen you in an aeon. Come and rain in spades. Tell us what it is that we look for.

Byron – testing new waters. Testing things that are to come. Testing out the shell of things. Never once believing, no. And here where the future is mapped in ancient parchment, there can only be one thing to do, and that is be in the middle of it.

Byron

Holding on, so as never to let go. Seeing the distance, so that our eyes do not blur. What is this thing that has no name? What is this retrograde motion in the heavens? Do we forward our desire to the next of place, next of whirlpool?

Byron – do you see yourself running? Do you see yourself in flight at some point? Why not, all is possible to you. And then, an intrepid adventure, one where you live. There is nothing more gracious than man of letters who has done something great.

A coursing through the hills, such that we don't care. A catching one by one, such that we don't care. A seething, a seething through the mist, such that we don't care. But where does the care come in – that depends on where it is.

Byron – are you with us? Are you the one to come, to arrive at the moment of salutation? There are things we must only do to keep the peace. And here, irregularities of grace, and all that will pass. Do not be afraid.

A feather that floats. Bringing all existence together in that one motion. We can stop and see it if we like. Shall we? Let's do just that. And then we can climber higher than before, on wings of mischief. Why don't we try?

Byron – are you alive? Are you the one to say, we can? Is there more to remember, here as in elsewhere? Here, as in the door of respite, come crashing, crashing for deliverance. What have we said, but all that is? What have we felt, but nothing at all?

Casting stones into the abyss – here we find ourselves, once again. And then, what we find, is of the roof of things. But there is no roof, to find or forlorn, but that is the way of it – the impossibility, but come as we may, we will find ourselves.

Byron – laughing through the years, your life stabled across a vast expanse. Something that was not together in any fashion, or any trope. We have seen you in many guises, and many turns of phrase. And here, we knew you as a sun.

Commiseration, you have left your life, but you have now seen what is beyond, and that high-lights the life we lead now. Can you coach us, but no, that is not the game? Each person finds out for themselves. And in that we are gracious.

Byron - coming to the speed of things, we see a route, something to takes to where we want to go. There is now a bliss factor that alleviates it all for you but that is okay, there will be a time for the rest. Do not wander through caverns unknown.

Aghast, and never seen. What we should only see in the dark. What we seldom visit, but not revisit. What is closest to us, but not harbouring fate. When the hem strays, when violence is the norm. And then there is life, in all its trepidation.

Byron – do you have sands on the wheel of it? Is yours a casting approach? I have never seen a rise such as this. I have never betokened the years, but what of that? I fear I will have the change of it. And then, living to be sure, we know when.

A fashioning of away! Going in for the remedy for it. Seeming not to care, nor envisioning things to be. I am left here, like a wastrel on the mire. Do not count on the well-spring, it only curtails the sensitivity of things.

Byron

Byron – do we climb the stairs at the same time? Is this what we must do to live our lives? Is there a mandate from the realms? The realms of sparkling and of fate? There comes a mas-sive abrasion, where knowledge seeks a redress.

We know how to pass the lest. Do you follow us now, my Byron? Come and think our way through things, that is the only way – the only way through. And then, with map in hand, and with flourish, we come to the mount of disdain. Yes.

Byron – Do you cling to it? This acceptance of the heart? This wisdom from the somatic? This disturbance in the weave? I have felt no more can be done, but this is not so. Much more can be done, and will be, in time.

Measuring with great sticks. Measuring so that the place is underwhelmed. There is now a wish that we continue, and so we will, with the blessing of all that is. Shying from the tasks at hand, we know of no other way.

Byron – does your sand break at the news? Does that which tailors the wind have you in sight? Do you gather all you are worth? Do you sense the same, and then have it confirmed? There is no wishing like the steel of it.

There are ways to be incensed, and ways not to be. Let us chose the latter, and then get down to business. The height of it is assured – the tail of it, is too. But what of the landing on the sea shore? The jump was high, but what of this?

Byron – do you curl your arm at the sight of it, does the dashing revolt leave us astounded? We have nothing left to deliver. We have nothing left, so let us proceed on tender-hooks, and know that place of our arrival well.

Constantly fading but never faded. The choice is clear, we must not fathom the deep for the sign of it. We must always rear our head in times of jovial unease. Come now, there is a sight that draws us on. What is it? We will see.

Byron – do you change yourself even now? Is this the intent of it? To remain in the race, and through the gate? I see things clearly, and then for change, cloudy. There is more than the tapestry to peruse. We must come on in fits and spirts.

A signal to the rest of us, we must toe the line of excess, and be the wandering of fireflies in morning light. Come and gather, gather the rose-petals as they fall – to this we give a solemn acceptance. An acceptance into things.

Byron – are you alive? Do you still dread the end? There is motion here, I can feel it. Never once riding, always walking – we must step through our shadow, and see it rebound. And just as we conquer, so we are there.

What was worth the rest, there was no other option. What was the sense we had to let it go? And here, there was fun in the trees, such that we could not find the way. And then, a chasm of light, the sort that finally finds a home. And well, anon.

Byron – letting go of the runes, that have as their transposition nothing more than the stones of yore. I have not found a single vantage point from which to see the sounds of your governing. Let us wander past this, shall we, and see the moat here too.

And here, a cautionary tale. Never leave the light on in the moonlight, nor never leave the door open when it is cold.

Byron

There are chances here to use our invective to catch a glimpse of all that is. The sun will shine.

Byron – much temper accosts the crowd, until the reigning lantern gives up the day. And here, much is said that cannot be unsaid – much puzzlement at the heart of it. And now, without the need to hurry, there is a testament written only for us.

Conscious of the time, we hear the heart at its core, and then, a solemn ritual that has not a crossing of the mood. There is now time to renounce all, and have as our dominion the acco-lades of a thousand years dreaming. Be there with us.

Byron – a new sense of old wells. We will find that thing that has no soul, and we will blow into to give it one. And then with the night so close, we will now see the sense of it, and let the time past in solemn duty.

Being at one with the sea – it is the only way to be. Being a sense to the eye, there is nothing yet to stand for. Be the listening, it will fill your nights. And here, mighty maestro, there longs to be a way to live here. We shall see, and then – well, yes.

Byron – a livery that joins at the knee. What we sensed could only happen in-extremis, but is now conducive in a mild state. Having just the right keystone, never living the life of it. Some-times we see the clouds in-absentia, and know things well.

A flourish that does not diminish the situation, but only enhances it. Will the daylight only slacken, or will it tighten? This much is at the foothold of it. This much is at the fjord. We have known for too long the mysticism of it all.

Byron – Happening again, but this time with the weathering of desire to incite us. And then, with catapulting resin, we come at full speed, through the arches that cool us there, back through the shaft of light that is the key. And then, home.

A disused flame that presents no danger. And here where we stagger on through to the other end, we see now what it is worth. We see what invites us to the journey of a life-time, and then back in time for biscuits and cake.

Byron – clearing the head, we are left to gather our own delays before they become delays, whistle in tune with the sea, or each walking step. The candles are here to excite the senses, in particular sight, but also hearing, not so much touch.

A whisper that does not leave a mark. Looking sideways, and through the gathering. There is a nice time to charge, to charge the hurrah! Do not be still here, there is no time. Only come when you want, there is ample opportunity.

Byron – catching a clasp, that has fallen from one the gatherers, and the returning it. There is now time to sit in deep repose, that for a while now has been impossible for us. And then, without fear, nor respite, there is a time to go for longing.

A semblance of the nothing of things. Listing down the road, full of the newness of the day. Casting around for something to do, but knowing the gauge of the window pane to be more than enough to see us there. Then we are through.

Byron

Byron – travelling through an impasse, there is a simple sign which directs the way – left or right, nothing more. You can go over, forward and through, but this is not recommended. Come to see the sign, come and witness choice.

There is nothing more than what we see. There is nothing more than what we have. And here, lasting in the sun, the catapult that sees us there, can no longer see the heights, as the depths. It works wherever though, and will take us there again.

Byron – a little kindness is what the trees envisage, envisage to the sweetness of things. Sometimes we wait, sometimes we go, sometimes the conditions are right, sometimes not. And then, with care, and a little bit of benevolence, we rest.

Swinging in between the rafters, there are tales of sweet delight. Where do they come from, these tales, we do not even know? There is a sense of the overall joy of them, but what is it that we seek? What is it that that jawline does not miss?

Byron – swimming through uncharted waters, we see what we have never seen. And here, where the nice and the assiduous come to together, there is a flame that no longer burns, ex-cept for one thing. It is a flame that still burns the heart.

Forests in the meantime, forests that harbour all we see. There is a never-ending ride that gives us the tension to carry on. We love our journey, but what of the rest? What of the need the stars have to gather up the dew, and see it through?

Byron - hanging on for life itself. Being prestigious in a school for the prestigious. Having the desire, but not expending anything more than what is needed. Being a hedonist in a stoic institution. Waving from the forearm, and never looking back.

Having the sense, and knowing it. Being perturbed, and seeing through it. Being off handed, and still winning. Having to deal life's hand, right in front. What can be the last thing we see? Forever in the breeze of things, rushing by.

Byron – are you the one to say, on the contrary! Are you whom the night gurgles free? There is a light coloured rose by the door, can you see it, and then get it, and then hand it too me? Such intensity is good in a man.

Laden with smiles from the top of things, an assurance takes hold. We know not from which part of the world the passage roles from, but here as in life, a dutiful concern reigns. There is silence, more than which can be set in any chiselled stone.

Byron – Casting forth, and through and around - there is nothing left to see here, nothing wondering through the hills, or up dale, or over fences – nothing around the limestone nor the treasures of time. Be one to see things through.

A clearing of the mess from the gathering of the night before – something to do, something to talk about. We have as the listening of the multifariousness of things, new fashioned oak, and solid sense floors.

Byron – cleaning things despite the tenderness. Having a like-minded friend, someone who you can see like you. The distance is not insurmountable. The rubble does not sting.

Having said that, all rubble stings, to a greater or lesser extent.

Catching things as they come. Desiring, but not seeing. Having the courage, having the where-with-all. There is a place, a place the wind does not know. And in this place, there is a wound of silver and broach. It is here where we find ourselves again

Byron – do you see the grass before you? It is here where the farmer tended to his cattle, and raised his children. How do I know? It is written in true blood, blood that never ceases. And it is here we must stand, and yes, make a stand.

Catching what is left. Catching the solstice through whatever is left. Whatever is the cause of our misfortune, we must find it, and massage it away, away from the looks that bind, and ste-reotypes that linger. We will never see his likes again.

Byron – shall we be that which comes last or first? In this there is a symmetry, we shall not fathom. And when the first white tiger has come, there lands a dream, a dream, that is so for the march, as it is for the day. This is it. Jump.

Seemingly like the rest of it. Surprising like the new measure of past adventures. And here, where the likes of the sky never diminishes its hold on us, we live, for another few days. And then, when we least expect, tomorrow, and the sun that projects.

Byron – Let nothing go! Let the file of life have its sway. The swag of it, is nearing its comple-tion. And then, casting the youth for the show, we know what is needed. Laughter, and tears. Greater, and larger than has yet to be seen. Well-done.

The feather that floats. Through the air, and onto the ground. Never once seeming lost or mis-guided. And when, when the treasure has its day, three is a likeness to the sun, the sun of day, the moon of night. Come and say hello, we will be pleased.

Byron – never believing, never knowing. Is this way of it – for each to determine for them-selves? Come and be that sky happy, such is the news of it. There are sands that do not tell the time! And here, where we gather nightly, silence, yes.

The singe where the candle fell, is that yours, mighty one? There are systems in the wind of it that know no season nor breath. And here, where the nuances are a little hazy, there resides the chance to battle on, till the end. We are in agreement.

Byron – the more we need to fight, the less we need to remain calm. The more we need to re-main calm, the less we need to find out what has happened. And in this marked remonstrance, there belies a truth – yes, and here it is!

Here and there, sprinkled partly and in whole, there lingers an extra place, that harbours no dream, nor place to sit. And here we stand, shoulder to shoulder, palms to palms. And then, before we have recourse to the tribe of denizen, away!

Byron – are you one to walk another step or two past where you are going? And then, do you turn with that special step, the step that lights up the night? This is all true, but what of the cascading waterfall that lets nothing through? We will see.

Byron

Watching the window pane for signs of life, watching the life scurry away. There is something to speak of now, that has less of the rainbow, and more of the sun. Less of the trading blows, and more of the withstanding all.

Byron – Running down that hill backwards, so as not to hurt ourselves. Having the stream to wade through, and then emerging on the other side. There is here, and now, something great, something we need, in times such as this.

Hastening, and then lavishing. Being fruitful, but not with avarice. Handing the straight back to the beyond, and then having it back yourself. There are times in amongst it, where the strength of the daylight is enough to remember us by.

Byron – come quick, and see the folds are in touch. There are things here, where the noisome and the brigade are want to fully entrench the stars in arbours of quiet, arbours of desire. Come quick, and see the trace of all that is.

A lot like the little we saw, in line with the hastening, of chaste and wintery eyes. In this there is love. In this there is the sentinel of fire that clears all around. Despite this, there is a gate of charming creations, who never seem to go away.

Byron – having a host of a time. Halcyon, indeed. And here where we love to be, here, where there is nowhere else quite like it, we sense the outreaches of fun will be had. And in this, nothing more can be said. Nothing else quite like it.

Shallow, and a foot beyond compare – there is work, and stones to attend to, and life in charge of all that is left. The diamond here ceases to trouble. But what of the starlit grandeur of things? What of that, as it echoes in wonderous times?

Byron – fetching more of the soles of our feet, than anything at all. Considerate and compas-sionate, never belittling, always chasing for the best, and here, where the stones of love show themselves on the steps of a wonderland – here.

Coasting for the right envelope to be found. And then, where love and loss have their twin announcements, there is play acting all-around. Is this the way it goes, on towards the flaying of the rice, and then nectar?

Byron – are you the one to see things anew? Are you the one to right the landfall before it falls? Is this what it takes, takes to bend the ship in half, and to see it splinter above? There are places unknown, and yes, we will find them.

Veering left, and veering right. This carriage has life. But now, we come around again, and listen intently, to the fabric of the stage. There are parts of life we do not understand, but that is okay, one day, we will build a monument to answers.

Byron – A vestige of the middle of it, that comes in squares and circles. There is now a hope we have, that what we have, is hope itself. And then, in-between, the rock and the table, comes to banish all who don't understand.

Having the sense to settle the score. Being what is, in truth, the stamp of approbation, there longs a very long breath, exhaled in full. And then without the slightest bit of care, we carry on, unto the hills and unto the way.

Byron – do you curse the day for its intractability? Do you wonder in streams of gold, streams of crimson? Can we still see the land from where we are? Cottoned as we are in deepest blue. I have one more thing to say to you – now go.

Byron

Fossicking through old book stores that never change their stock. Being right on the furthest part of the wall, and only coming back. The difference between me and you is small, one of degrees. And then a smile, and a return to life.

Byron – much is said of you, do you believe it? Do you believe the attention still? That is worth a mountain of salt, to wear away the days, the sun, and all the rest. We will only be conscious never to sail again. And when we are clear, once again.

There are times in amongst it when the arrow of fortune comes to bare. And it is here where we must jump that little higher. Most of what comes in the meantime is an oration (an oration of sorts) that never tempers soil, nor lost belief.

Byron – saddling up until we find the next piece of news. Saddling together, and not folding an inch. Being smart, and being ostentatious. Together we lie, together we wait. And here, where to sample is a thing to enjoy, again, life. And again, Life.

Causing a commotion, there are differences in the night, differences, we can't fight, and here a sort of commotion, that lets linger the heart of things, back down to its natural resting place. What is this? Love shirked? We will come.

Byron – often-times there are things we don't understand – things that make us cringe, or are obtuse, or have as there starting point the mire, or the fumbling of cards. In this there is a way through. All we must do is try again.

Considerate to the very last. What is it that we have beside us? What is it that blows no horn, nor mist to bully once again? Gather around, we have something to say – we will make it through. And when we have done this, here a whisper of order.

Byron – The time is right for us, my Byron. The time is right to let the cataclysm show itself, such that we might believe once again in times to come. There are letters that do not arrive, where most do. And here, we can know only silence. Here.

A sort of thing we can understand. And in this thing, there are roles by plays-with-in plays, and roundings, and shortenings, and being verbose, and leaving the last thing till last. And here there is a chance once again to the best we can be.

Byron – withholding nothing, we fight for what is the daylight on our skin. There comes a chariot, that roles no vector, and has spite beside the ruins. Let us be the front of it, not on the side, nor the rear. Pleasantries are for the noble amongst us.

Holding on, we see no incentive for the window to be opened. But here, in the wind and rain, we gather a new persistence, one that heralds no pain, nor worry of any sort. And then, when we come again, a sense that things will right themselves.

Byron – testing every fibre of the way of it, we come to another junction. And here, the times are like an open display of what is most alike. Don't be the one to shed so soon, there can only be one thing to do, and that is wade through, and beyond.

Mismatched, and terrified. We come to the crossing of life once again. And here where the nearly faded, and wholly faded, came to rest, there is a new found deliverance, that has no sheen on its back, nor elbow on its sleeve.

Byron – coming close, we know now what to expect. There are differences in amongst the sand – differences that hark back to a year and place that has no wind nor placation to unwind. There is something we must choose. We will, and then see.

Most importantly, the gathering of rose petals is such like a most pleasant domain. What should we do, but hark back to the memories of a life time? There are sayings that have as their digressions the tinkering of fireflies, fireflies in August.

Byron – such is the way of it – such is the plan and the abode. What the night will not have. What the stance will unhinge. Come now, fear not, there is moisture in the middle of it. And here, where the dust is like wildfire, we are steady in our case.

Ideal for the departed – new things, old wares. Come now, there is no time, there is no time for the simplicity of things. Do your best, and do it well, and yours will be the lightning on the rod. This much is clear. And then, without thought, a sort of release.

Byron – catching the ramshackle and the room, we measure ourselves by the steam we keep, and the likelihood of tomorrow's embrace. We sing, but not in key. We laugh, but only in the middle of pauses. And each laugh ascends to something special.

Creeping inside for a dance – a one and only, forever riled, forever going to it. And there, there is noise and adumbration, but nothing we can sooth with a strong stroke of the pen. When we see ourselves, we laugh – there is nothing more to it.

Byron – wishing for the half of it, and not going selfish for it. There is now a mellow task at hand, that switches on the cane sticks as deftly as the runner in silk flies to the finish. We will wait again, till the end of things – and then, away!

All in, or all out – almost, or all outside. And there, in the distance, a swinging type of things, that has no need to travel in outward motions. I see it coming from outside the sphere, the sphere of flight, where every bird learns its craft.

Byron – having what is seen as the truth of things, being certain, and then away. The minds eye. The teeth that gnash. The eyes that blind. The hair that scurries down. The fingers that pinch – owwh! What is this we say, we say yes, and then turn.

A climb to the very heart of things. A racing that does not believe in tales nor wares. What we listen to, is not the fog of ages – nor the dandelion, Byron, but something else. There is a tributary we must not forget. It is here, and away.

Byron – away, and away with it! And then, with cheerless speech, and wonderment in the eye, there transposes good from evil, night from day. And hay, there is the time it takes to worry the few, to worry the ramshackle and the dice. Yes.

Arriving in the middle – but where is that? Arriving in first tier, first place – but where is that – simply arriving, before we have touched the wall, even. Before the simplicity of it all wanders down the archway. There is a mess no one can clean. We hope.

Byron

Byron – clinging to things, like the sand in the hour glass. Like the never-before-seen tide. Like what is best in all of us. Like what is not, and what is so. Rummaging up the granite from the cellar, and using it to extend the house. We will follow.

Following on from the garden, we seek no inclement weather. This would only warm the shoulders of want-to-be classists. And here where the stifling solution is near at hand, we take a digressive motion, to once again feel the life, as it pulses.

Byron – keep the stoic store of life at your finger-tips, and reach for it at every opportunity. There are mustangs a foot, as wild as the laymen in need. We whistle past the commotion, and have as our salt, the testing of water-led fate.

Holding hands with the newness of it all. We soon face a belittling. What is that, I hear you ask? It is a strange and fruitful occasion, this, but they essentially mean nothing. But why the song and dance? We will see in time.

Byron – everlasting, never vanishing, always on the plateau, and here, where the noise of it drowns, there comes an infinitesimal delay, one we can treasure if we like, or not, it is up to us. We set the ball in motion. Till then – hay, charades.

Blistering, and feeling the sound through our knees. There are times when the dance is more for the October of things, than for anything else. And when we stride clear, we do so with a single thought - 'forward'. And then listen for the beyond.

Byron – having the sense to be in the tail of it. Having the sense to be what's more. Being selfish, but not too soon.

Having the heart, and seeing it through. Being tremendous, but not letting on. Being that thing that is not concerned.

Having a sense that the wall will not fall. A feeling that the stone is here to help. Gather your beliefs, while they are still in tune. And then, without the slightest fear, move through, and then allow yourself to be whisked away.

Byron – moving ahead, never once tiring, never a pinch too much, or too little, never saying it is enough, always believing, in things and in people. The dance is one to remain so, and here, there is time to wonder, and wonder still.

Glasses of ambrosia to raise for the toast. Little bits of left-over bread, to be eaten with break-fast. And then, a new type of silence, one that doesn't hear even itself. The sense we have that things are not infinite. The belief in all things.

Byron – are you wise enough to see? To see, the sea? And then a round of pleasurable asides, asides that have only their tails to decide upon. And here, where things are calm, the might of sound and trawling's for air, come, and are assured.

Frequency of visits to the gallery – not more than can be expected – frequency of swims to prove a point – extra times to be displayed. The tempest does not own you, Byron, the tempest only owns ourselves, in these times, and the next.

Byron – do you march that way down. That way down with accoutrements. And then the sail is set. The repairs to the barge gather pace, and soon we will be off. We cannot be ones to let the vessel run free. There is much to be done.

Byron

Having something to say, but not saying it. Being of the opinion, but not giving in. The vector and the mean. There is a change of carriage here, where we never let go. We never let go, and then for the time, we usher in merriment, and then the night.

Byron – are you set in your ways? Do you wish for something else? Is there more to this than meets the temperament? The distance for the settlement. An age ago – wouldn't you agree? And then the tails are here, but what of the tales?

What is never put to tether. The strength to have the light shine. And then, when the solstice comes, there will be a new mood, one that doesn't have the tenacity of other guardians. The type is of sun, and her embrace. There is nothing more to say.

Byron – having the tangential surround us, and then going for the load. A sort of round-a-bout way, but that is okay. Not knowing, not staring, not being fierce, being fierce, and not knowing why. The upshot is this – the clouds are not here to envy.

Using the key to open the door. Such a simple thing, but so complex. There is missing here, the night of mistakes, that takes as its guise the sand and the repartee. The moisture too, we must not forget. Come and see.

Byron – the air and the wind, the sound, and the newness of it. Come for the flight of it. Something that leaves a mark as it furrows. Never one to see again. Never one to be for the land of it. Come, do not dice, there is here what is needed.

Being betrothed to the word. Is it enough to send sparks of contumely through the aether, never to return? We will be forgiven. And then, without favour, nor care, the mast which holds this boat steady, languishes forward, and we are away.

Byron – nestled in close, we find time to give the journey one last hooray, and then, in chance of pursuit, a change in things, that has us basking in open air. Give the sense to change things around. And then, a sound of breath.

Being at one with the sense of it, as we come a little closer. There is now the sort of life we never expected. This life, has as its base, the simple and the urbane, what have we said, but more of the same. Give the reticent the chance to be.

Byron – issuing forth the need of all strides, there is a statue of Minerva that stands directly in our path. We don't move it, we just walk past, in greys and hirsute yellows. What is more, we come to let things go, so here goes!

Costing what is dearest, the entry price seems munificent to all of us, and here, oh here there is a sort of registered aplomb, that wages steps to take, and steps to stop taking. There can we be in the circle again – that time has passed.

Byron – resting forth, without having the chance to be that way again, we have now a schism of boldness, to the wellspring. Come now, we will endeavour just to be. And what is that, just to be? We will shovel ourselves a rainbow.

Given the sport of the intransigent, we must continue on. And here, most kind, and in need of repatriation, there comes a holler down the alley-way. A sound that has as its fibres nearness, and direction. Come now, this will suit.

Byron

Byron – Being in touch with all that moves. Being the ones to say, yes, I will. Always standing on the rooftops when making a noise. Standing up to things, before they become rife. The little more we know, the greater the chances we have.

Gladdening to see the sights, mighty England dominates. And here where the sands do not touch the glass, the emptiness of the vase does not go unnoticed. Come now, we must not linger. To linger means to unravel the gist of it.

Byron – being the life of it, and not sitting down. Being that which has no fault, and then lying in wait. The message is a simple one – do what you do best, and do it well. And then, like a meal on a stick, come for the caution of it. You will bear fruit.

A sort of miserly tribute that has no sound, nor want to tribute. And here, where the mystery runs deep, there are more of the things that turn, than burn. And now, when the comfort is rightly switched, the twitch of land lays itself under.

Byron – the next of it sures itself against the land, and does so without compunction. And then, with noise and display, there comes the sentinel delight – something we all should partake of, if we have the time. And then in agreeance then – fast.

Hanging on to see it. Those on their deathbed see true. And then without the rock, nor the cradle, their begins again, the disdain of the morbid. And here when things are bright, the testing of winder cold is never in doubt. We have found.

Byron – a sort of static that doesn't know the left, for the right, nor transposing the weather on the tempest slate.

Come and be the way of it, you will shine. And now with eddies of triumph, we swing in tune to the solstice. And yes, then.

Holding out for more, but content with less. A makeshift raft that tallies journeys like the wind. And then, where the landfall is like a boot strap, there comes a rallying cry – we will come, and we will secede. And that would be that.

Byron – seeing like it is somebody else's. And bounty that knows no rite. A sense that rings true. What we thought was never in the way. And then, with the moisture content reaching a high, there is nothing out of the ordinary.

Fixing the post before it bends right over. Being shy of the second bite. Being one to happily fall over, especially after a line. Coming close to the heart of it, such that the maze is in the wood. The wood is in the maze. There is now time to consolidate.

Byron – do you sense the upcoming stanza, to be uplifting, or demoralising? Do you have a feeling that the book will swim, or flounder, your latest one that is! And then, much to our sur-prise, the fence-line has and upside, and here it is!

Congratulating the time we spent, in lieu of the new sporting grace. There are chances to be once again. Chances to send a well wish to a friend before the end. And then, when the nice-ties we seek, are ravelled in wonder, we will find again.

Byron – do you find yourself in amusing situations with those you have loved before? There is nothing more invigorating than a caesura in the wind. And here, where the noise we make is only in proportion to distance we are away.

Byron

Catching a hold, on the face of it, such that we never let things fold. And here, where the heart is in line with the gods, there is now a falcon to needs surpassing. Come now, the fault is not our own. The fault is in the weave of things.

Byron – lasting like it was possible. Having a solid base on it. In the threads of desire, there is a plaintive refrain. And on that stand, nothing more can be said. And then without the transparency to wonder, there comes a time for rest.

Loving that which comes next. And now, without the departed to keep us company, there is more of yellow precision than a dark one. But what is left of us, but the fielding of questions that have no answer. And there is more to say here.

Byron - are you the one to be in a hurry? Is this the sense we have? When begetting has the ire of the commonplace. Do we sense the fill of all that is, and then the dire of the makeshift rain? Fill me up, and let me travel. That is all I ask.

Consideration to the well of ages. There is an arc to this bell, that has as it motion the sky and the stars. Do not begin a retrograde motion, it could be something we would be remiss about. Come closer there is a lag in the seam of things.

Byron – coming into it – feeling a loss, but going forward. Seemingly intrepid, we catch that glow, in untold ways. There is never enough to keep going, but we keep going. And here, where the standstill starts, there is a coffin to fill.

On our knees, can you see? On the very fibres of what is called enough. And then when things are like things, we can come further forward that we ever thought possible. Without the desire to drive the carriage, there is no carriage.

Byron – are you there, do you wish for the moves we make to be half hearted, can you triple our need, and have us fenced in? There is like an untold bastion, that rings in scales, scales of abandonment. What is this I hear you say?

Breaking the glass to see what's next. Hearing the stage as it rattles by. Being one to choose the cacophony. And here, where the land is firm, and the trees are rounded, there is always a chance of the penumbra of things. Here we stand.

Byron – have you seen the latest play by the latest playwright, there is much to be pleased by. And here, there is a time to be aghast, and appalled. And when we are through with the lining of things, a conscious awareness of the plate that casts.

Witnessing the very back of the well-spring, we see ourselves loved and not dispersed. And then, in touch with all that is, we can once again find that thing which is normally lost, but lo, it is now found. Catching rain to drink.

Byron – wishing the well well. And it was like the raiment had stirred a leaf, and was now a different colour. And then, as if by magic, the sterner stuff of the world had quickly made its mark, and then retreated to find solace in the things that bind.

Crossing swords with the best of them, clawing back with the worst. And now there is a hand-someness to it, that we know. What have we got but the load to live by? And that startling life, we are proud to lead. There is a journey ahead.

Byron

Byron - rustling in the fate of it. There are numbers by which to go by. This will happen at this point, and that will happen at that point. And here, where the tom foolery gets past the point of no return, we will linger with no regret.

Having to see things twice, being unable to roll the dice, being that greater part of a secondary skill – translation it all started there, didn't it Byron? And then when things called, you followed, even though you had an inkling of what would happen.

Byron – singing in tune with it. Harking back to see the chorus. Harking back to be something more. And when our turn comes, there rises a ransom over things, over things that have no jollity. And the answer – there is none.

Gouging, and having what the stones throw, having what we most need. Being the challenge, and the time it takes. There is something more to all of this. Something more, and yet something we don't understand. We will follow.

Byron – clasping on for the ride. We see it coming, but do not see the way. The way forward is what we need, but that is shown to be a trouble a curse. But what do we do to ride the curse open to the sending of winter missives?

Cascading in full view of the water, and here, where the loading on docks has a certain rhythm, things will come to pass that have as their load the worrying of autumnal digressions. Come and be a proud father to the flanks of our remiss.

Byron – a kind of lucky grin crossed his face. And it was the upside of so much, and so much in-between. And cuticles that never faced the wind would come from their hiding place, and then relayed back again, such is their want.

Having no side to trim. Having the wondering home, that marks the exit and entry of the man of letters. Come and see the sign posts of the new way to live. Forever boxing and clouting the cornerstones of this life.

Byron – there is a touch and a wink at the new found disarray – something we can only get a grasp at, very, very, slowly. And then, when the march stops, there is a visible machine Ada is working on, and that is something surprising.

Being tired, but carrying on. Having the sequence of things, but not yet down. Being wanting in a strange land – strange enough, it is thought, that we should walk the way we do, or talk the way we do. But listen, we will come again.

Byron – hanging on close, there is no choice. And there, where things ought to be, a nuance that readies the time caught in seething embrace. Do not tumble, the night will make headway, until the day of slumber moves in. Watch, and see.

And there in the embrace of one piece to another, there is a warmth to the sound of it. And what we thought was an attack of senses, is now nothing more than a conflagration of snow. Come to the wish we have, that sentience is all around us.

Byron – Having the courage, not to be of the rampart – and here there is a nice way to be, that reigns in gulfs and tenure. And here, where the pipe glows the strongest, a heaven made banquet, that oldest is the way of it, come again for love.

Byron

Sign posts, that linger, in sempiternal gloom. But what emerges, but the most effervescent life. And now, we have no thought for the mildest form of subreption, nor what is most at stake, without the dreams of men, and women.

Byron – just having the scale of it, to climb that little bit further up, and away. And now, without the need to be, and to want, there is a silence that rings only in our ears. And then, what do we say when we are there – 'now'.

Having something special to say, but not saying it. Being of belief, but not knowing why. And then when we are through, the sights come clouding in. What do we mean by this? There is nothing worth knowing here, but we will continue.

Byron – do you sit with Virgil at your side, plumbing the mysteries of the after-life? Now that would be an adventure. I have no faith in the whales and wiles of a spiral time elaboration, but we must continue, so we will – yes.

Casting a net, seeing where it goes, loving the life of it, all till it goes. A random simplicity em-barks with us, and here, where the sand is of the beach, nary a moribund look will stop us. But what of the here and now? It will suffice.

Byron – are you mellifluent, king of the word? Do you scatter yourself within your books, and the emerge with words of fine standing? There is more of the cost here than we could know. But what of the spite of it? We will gain a rich harvest.

Magnanimous to the last, and with a special touch, one that turns words to gold, and then back again. Please be so taken with these words I give to you. They are specially made, to enter your oeuvre – please take them where you will.

Byron – a simple ransom for you - your words, or your life, which would you choose? I would choose both, leaning towards your life. Sustained reasoning, and then a bunch of clay. We have felt it, and look what it has brought us.

Catching a sight of it, the wonder at its mist. Clawing at the seam of things, and knowing only one solution. There is a new phase to proceed on, and before it is here, we languish it stalls – spits and spats. Come now, we are from.

Byron – do you deliver on the main sail? Do you state yourself a happy tribe? Is this what we should do, for happiness and plain? Do not say what is yet to be said. It is already written down, and cannot be replaced. Be a vanguard to fate.

Looking sideways, and never a glimpse after that, there is time to roam, and time to roar. Being of that certain flavour, that transposes as it uplifts, there is a taint that has not the defiling reminiscent of the last. There are two things to choose from!

Byron – landing in the space of it, there comes a languorous night, that has no need of the sand, nor the light. Come for the certainty of dreams engage in other shapes and forms. There is a little bit of toe in the temperature. And then we say, yes.

Having the whisper become true. And then, having the tempest come through. There is nothing left to do, except one thing, and that is prise the window away from the dawn. Do this, and all will be well. Or else!

Byron – hoping to hold on. Hoping for the rest to remain still. There is like a sense that the trees will not fall, not yet at least. Be the tremendous sound the comes from the gut, and lulls in emotionful existence. Come now, and between.

Is there enough to be sending our state to lighter shades, where transitions are made in ear-nest. There comes a chance for rain. There comes a new fairy to dance the ceiling of our sor-row. Come now, time to eclipse, and time to rise.

Byron – less heart, more steel – less steel more heart. We are left to do that thing by halves – do not squander the rinse for the hills. There is now a thoroughly intact simile to inspect. Do not save the lonesome the time. Just a thought.

Being incensed, to see the land as it lay, lay before us. Never conceding an inch, we come to the sail pitch with all out rub. Never sense the maelstrom for what it is, which is strength itself, from noble partitions. Yes, a service.

Byron – There are things in the midst of it that we do not dare. There are people who have as a ratio the night. And when the Goliath rumbles through forever, there comes a mighty sem-blance. Where are we now? We cannot tell.

And now, like a fanfare, the mist is all encroaching. We don't come for the rain; we can leave that out. We come for the wishing of stranger things, that never say I do, and have the whis-pers on their life intact. What about that!

Byron – can you see me, from where you are? Is that the thing about the inlet, and the eddies of motion that come? Do try to be a walker in a strange land, there is nothing wanting about that. Come now, there are trees to coach.

And when we snaffle ourselves a right sense of the wrong delight, there is a chance we have to settle down and be at comfort. There is here a new way to be in old climes. Watch me now, I come for the taste of blended things.

Byron - a missing piece, that has no jibe to weather, nor mystery to tell. What have we come to, this world and I? What have we striven for, this world and I? I will not be the wicker man in the staging of mess. I will only be the show itself.

Hoping against the wall of it. We love what you are doing, you may persist. Be the manager of something important, and yours will be the sky. Do not have as the template anything other than this. We will satiate ourselves.

Byron – are you climbing through the wreck? Is this what we do, now and forever? I am the nestle bee, that harbours the way we talk, and speaks the way we act. Is this way we proceed? Through the tempest and the squall.

Having the strength, and seeing it through. There is now a keepsake inside us all, that when pressed, leaves nothing to the squall. And here, where the softest noise carries great weight, there is a sound victory against the night.

Byron – do you tremble at the thought of it? Is that what we have come to? And now, to rico-chet off the found and square, there is a long-lost dream, one we had over ten nights ago. Do you believe it? Can it be found?

A sort of card, that floats down to the ground with ample ease. And then when the earth shud-ders in the distance, we come once again to the place of perseverance, and know it for the first time. Do not find your way here, there is no time to lose.

Byron – catching the loudest part of it, only to be silenced by the wind. There is a time and a place that has not yet existed. And when they come into being, they will only exist for a short time, and then go out of existence again.

On the horizon, we known what must be. It is not up to us to decide, but we carry on regard-less. Come and see a play Byron – maybe a Moliere, if that is your pleasure. The rectified and the motionless, there are things to do, people to be.

Byron – watching for a sign of it. Watching for the trade. There is a sort of closeness in the weave of things. Do not herald the dawn, she will come. Of her own accord. Not-with-standing the cord that binds each of us to the wheel.

A magic type of game, where all the players line up, and have their pulse ready, and then, one two three, on your set, and go! A certain form of entertainment. What have we forgotten, but nothing, what have we felt, but the trepidation of what comes next?

Byron – having what we know to be a time of it. There are many ways to look at it. Firstly, we can see ourselves in the bluff, and know the tempest has no fuel to list by. Secondly, there is a lancing of the courage of things. Impossible. These two things.

Having something to go by, that has no need nor favour. And then, the dressage that knows only itself. There can only be what there is. There is the chamber and the mass. Tribulation, and festive cheer. What is left is nothing but all.

Byron – Coursing to the minds eye, the horse rushes into life. Comes out of a dream, and fashions into something else. Never believed we could, only to say, apology accepted. The test is in the wind of it, without which there is no rhyme.

What have we come for, but that which is nestled into the fabric of things. What have we be-lieved in but the shore line and the sand. What have we needed most, but a sternness that has not been lacking. We will try again.

Byron – sense without respite. And new time to gather old things. What is it that fumbles us through? The sequence of events that leads to our calling. We have found a way through, through the mist and through the willows – a way through.

Burrowed in, and not giving an inch. A sort of air that does not move in any direction. Heady for the last of it. Drawing on all our reserves. A nice touch that does not go unremembered. And then, despite the heat, a saving grace.

Byron – are you the one to run in palatable whimsy - down, and up again? Do we have some-place left to go? Is it time, already? The course to these events is laden with lead. Have we been to see elongated portrait? It hangs past us.

Smouldering, and leaving your mark, Byron. There are chances the shine, and chances to be one with the wind. But in the middle of it, frenzy, and never foreseen departures. I have only one thing left to give, and that is the tail of my spine.

Byron – are you sure of yourself? Do you pine for ages gone? Does your fashion extol the world? Have the hope we all have that things will reply. And then, when things are terrible, and we cannot find a glancing rod, safety, and retreat.

Pushing the boundaries of sense, the sensibility of things comes to pass. What have we thought, but the stones that do not throw. Come and be one with the crowd, there are things we will be able to do. Do not be one to roar at the lopsidedness of it all.

Byron – cautionary tales. Look to the life, and ask, would you pursue it? Of course you would – you have to do something, after-all. There is no better way to play the motive trance. Come with us again, there is a bee that flies for thee.

Effervescent and starkly, we have our need at flight, but there is a little and a lot, to under-stand, which neither have come to pass. So, we shovel the embers through the accompanying wall, and then, let our fears dissipate.

Byron – are you in the fabric of dreams, now Byron, is this you role – I haven't dreamt of you yet, but neither should I, visiting township after township, never being soul to soul. I have as a guiding buoy, you Byron. This much is sure.

Governing with steel, your Lordship never varies. And his domain? We never would have thought to think in plaintiff release. But that is not the holding of barriers still. So come, we have thought that our days not to be numbered.

Byron – liking what we see, feeling the terrace come down. Opening up, and then falling again. Being alone, and seeing straight. Should we endeavour to be more in-tune with life? There is nothing more exhilarating than this. Share what you believe.

Paul Fearne

Higher than the highest promenade. Seeing things that join into one. There are no distances more digressive. Forming an image from the depths, from the newest part of tomorrow. And when we find ourselves again, a silence that does not remit.

Byron – do you love it when we sail? Do you love it when the race comes down, down the line? We speak here of a swimming race, in the grand tradition. We all have our races – mine is to walk, what is yours, as we speak?

And then, a simple thing, one that does impress overtly, but only in the middle of the world in which we live. Come now, we are allowed a nuance to filled from time to time. And here where the last is not the end, there comes a stable, to facilitate.

Byron – What is the path in the jungle all about. What we see is more in love with the goings on of fate. This much is necessitated by the dawn. Come we will not show levity where there is none. We are proud to say yes to all who reside here.

A constant feature, that never lets go. Somebody to tell, what is for. And then in the strange-ness of succession, winter, and a glow of warmth. This is what we seek, beyond time and be-yond despair. See to it, we will find a way.

Byron – having the sentience to be able. We walk the future, and only now, come to our sens-es. I sense the way to go is this way, and then travel it ourselves before the sun break, and the trials of the late-night walk. We will come.

Having the sun on our backs, and being able to do as we need. Foremost in chanceless mo-ments, utter morning bliss, can we see for more? An industrious circumstance, relies heavily on the perpetuity of instability of the fragrance.

Byron – containing all that is. A raining frost, that has the soul as a necklace. Not to be in the forest after dark. Not to sink again, before time. Not to languish still, and still breathing. There are loops, loops that see themselves in night's dispel. Yes now.

Costing nothing less than all. Costing what can never be found. There is a time that heralds each passing day, like a fashion at whim to the whimsical. I have not seen much at bay, or much in the ruminations of a king.

Byron – having heard of so much, I came to look, and there, in the distance, a man in Napole-on's carriage. Do we weep, no. But have we seen all we can? No, indeed not. There are win-dows that look out to the sea, and we have found them.

Coming into contact with the might and territory of the stars, there is a semblance of hope in the mystery of all that is now. And see, when, the accoutrements of desire, never flare as they flare for the life of it. It is like this, always.

Byron – do you come in the motion of things, that stay as they have signifying armour? Is this what we seek in time with the shallow depths of yore. O, snore, come and be a blistered base, and we will see things till their vanishing point.

What we cannot dismiss, is enough to laden a trapdoor of simplicity. And then, without the cold, without the nearness of winter sundry, there comes a hope and a dream, and everything that is, is to us, and when!

Byron – featuring nothing less than what we thought. There are times to labour, and times to feel the motion of things deep inside. There is nothing there we can be listless by. We have at our hearth and might the seeds of a thousand turnings.

Having the fiasco, and knowing what is right about it. Believing in the solstice, and having the acumen to make it happen. Voracious, and in the between of things. Never quite knowing when the next blow is coming from.

Byron – launching into sadness, but with much delight. There is a time for calling a wince a dredge. There will be no more to it, to the vantage point of time itself. And now, to the region of the soul that permits the dance to come!

Moisture in the halo, we should attend to that. And there it is, sempiternal and derided, long sought, and half way dazed. And there, a new sense to obtain the wonder of the past. Come now, and have as your saying something special.

Byron – looking in, never quite knowing, knowing where to look. Have as a scribe your next of kin, and then do not seek to harbour your redress. There is no time to see the load, the load full of partitions that will go for the weight.

A hazard that needs no renouncing, that needs no hard and soft emplacement. Come to see things as they are. There is no time for wonder here, only insight, and all that is. Come to be for the mess of it, there is a certain solace.

Byron – are you keen to seek new ground? New bastions, new ways to tread. There is only now, the whispering of daylight hours, that come as feed for the nature of what makes us dear. I will not tell of any other thing.

Byron

Having what is needed in the crisis. Being alone, but continuing. Being steadfast, despite! What we thought was in error, is just the wind – a wind that blows up from the north, and then up our spines. We will continue.

Byron – I see your fear, and know that it languishes in solid refinement. Do not call us what you will, we are here to serve. And then without any part of road wet, we will travel indecently so. Do not hurry, the turn is for the best.

Gaining in momentum, we savage the tide as it seems to us. We come to no impasse as it stands. And there, the air, comes in triplicate bravado, never gaining, never waning. Help us now, there is time to see things abiding.

Byron – do you swim against the tide? Is there a measure in the side of it? Do we come to fulfill the cry of our ancestors? Is this what we have in mind, all of the way, but half as hearted. We will not stop, for any one, or anything.

Holding on, gathering grace. There is a new turn of speed, one that encounters no embrace. The sense we have to continue will only be that thing that does not settle. And in being so, there is nothing left to give as emotion or talent.

Byron - do you tend to your dotage? Is this the first time you have seen it, for nary two hundred years? There is nothing like this story of yours in gulp and splendour for more than it takes to carry a load. There can only be what is left.

Harking back to days of yore there is a scorch to remind us of what you were. Do not renounce the slumber as it calls to us. There comes more than what completes the cycle. Mischief and assailing with the nicety of utmost regalia. Life is yours!

Paul Fearne

Byron - being withstanding, and having more to say. Hoping that the treasure found will not be lost. And here, where the miscellaneous and the true, strengthen the resolve, a new breed of dissonance comes, one to give great pleasure.

Hoping against hope, the pregnant pause in the sophistry, knows no bounds. And here, listening carefully, here is a new taste for the climb ahead. Never believe in what is not true. And then, together, we march as simplest few.

Byron – in a rush, we see ourselves going, going for the night. But where is this, and where will it take us? Where is the letter that guides the way? There is pinning where there should be salt. There is a harvest that we need to partake of.

A glad start to the season. If it is spring, we know where we have come from. But to be in truce with the embers never lasts. But that is okay, we have sheltered from the storm, and now it time for the jovial, and the wit. This is what we had hoped for.

Byron – be as you please. There is no rest for the time-being, and here, where things seem strange, and negligible impact has occurred. And then, an honour to be had. What is worse is that dreams are filled with stone, and then away.

Who comes here – who dares come here? There was sleep to be had for no-startling. And then a sort of away stroke that left us winded. I cannot see the day of. It comes, but what of the dream. It will be had again – and again.

Byron – littered with scores of unknown origin, can you feel the way of it? It is as if we had blown off track, and never regained our direction. It is as if our tails were too much. We will never forget it – never forget what was to be.

Having a smooth transition, living in the now. We find not that which contains us, but that which makes us flourish. And then, like a time that doesn't cringe, but only grows, to ancient size, and then reaches, back again into something more.

Byron – loving with passion to the last. You have not the weather of it, nor the simple phase of rounded out brevity. There is here a new sense, to be faultless in ambition, and arriving too late. What have we said we will be – but all?

A figure of speech that rings a set of roses, and holds to the day. I am one that never lets go, but am here only on the periphery. I am with what is needed, despite my plea (and fun) with the world. We soar, on the wings of tide.

Byron – are you one to sleep again, are you one to relish the sun in disguise (the night)? Are you one to feel that is right, and that is time? We will fight for the backstage, and the feeling that triumphs the wheel!

It is like we never were. It is like the sound of the sky meeting the horizon was too much, and then, we looked again, and saw our way clear. There are mirrors here, things that blind. We have only the clearing of the rod.

Byron – having a hunch and seeing it through. There can only be the chanceless unbridled sanctity of the light. We are guided, but we guide. Someone who knows the time of departure. Next coach to Venice.

Let us begin again. Let us say, the air is cooling, and the mystery never leaves. We see through the ancient settling, like a handsome man, never wanting to flay the life between our eyes. Come now, we are here to stay. Now let us roam.

Byron – are you a sage? Do you have acclaim to be, and then silence? Is this what they say is the chime, and the lance. Never out of pace, we come for the frivolity. Now that we have sense, we come for the inclement amongst us.

Hauling the luggage through the rooms, there is nothing to set foot on. There is now a whistling sound through the air – but what do we say? And what do we do? Can we be like the rest, and miss our fondness for the ramp?

Byron – the ever-vigilant mode of delight that some are prone to, sees us sending the nous through the world, the sky and into the heavens. Do we dice here? Do we settle on cadences that have no rhyme? There will be a task.

Hunting like we were the hunted. And now, with four score and thirty. We have never seen the likes of this. An ancient tree which transcends time, and has as the vehicle of incision, just like the testing strength. Never be late. It is worth the wound.

Byron – The rest is yours, use it well. Have that which is strong, come for what is kept. Be in-transigent whenever you can, except when love takes hold. And there, in the window, a reflexion. We suffer much, but how much? That is for the signs to tell.

What have we found, but all that is? What have we lost, but again, all that is? There comes a temporality that knows only strength. And here, where we lay the burden down, there are pleasures that only the dreamer can conceive.

Byron

Byron – sitting upright as if in a trance. Being subdued no more. The outrageous fortunes of fate. We will see it through, come now, we must. But what of the time between us? There is no time, no playing on the Lyre.

Setting the sun on fire. Belligerent, but ill informed. Loving the school of things. Having the dice, and being willing to use them. Not drenching, just filing. Interested in what comes next. A little too hard, not hard enough. Ticklish by design.

Byron – do you wander through halls decorated with gold leaf, and then on to lakes made of crystal? Is this where we seek you, when things are grim? I have not made the township my own, not for many a long year. We will fight.

Festivities, that run in a sideways motion. Something that lasts the distance. Ruminating on the complexities of things. Being intrepid, but not losing sight – sight of what is, and what is not. There will come a beautiful sound.

Byron – looking the wrong way. Looking forwards, but not backwards. Having something spe-cial to say, and saying it at the appropriate time, and the appropriate place, to a large gather-ing. What is next, I hear you ask? Much.

Having the right culture to get you there. Being a mess, but having the right to look hirsute. And then, without care, nor rhyme nor respite, there rises a milestone in the fibre of things. The time is past for games. And now – what now?

Byron – often looking after the sentential structure, never baring to say well, or oft, or nary. There are children that have as their favourite things books, and with them, all that brings. A sort of cloud, that dances, and never plays the sky of it.

The message we have for you, is one of calm, and deep solace. Can we live this way, when our brethren list from one shore to the next? I hope we can. But what of the life thread, that keeps us breathing, and heaving in equal measure?

Byron – I ask you, once again, have you seen the day? Does it rest in your palm? Are there flowers for you? Do you tempt the seasons with blossoming too soon? Never be one to try as this, the keepsake washes through. Hang the release.

Catch a hold of us, Byron. Catch and do not let go. There is a figment at the wind, so let us dance. We dance at the sight of it, so let us dance. Be sure not to placate what we see; it is not enough fill the writhing for scores to come.

Byron – at carnival did you stay with the flying of fish, and then the coming into the being of a namesake. There is now the holiday to the stars. We will fashion, what is In line with duty. I have now a configuration of speech for you.

A new way to pitch it. We show our limestone heart to all who care to look, and watch there faces show astonishment. Astonishment, at what? Purely at the limestone. A heart has never been released that way before.

Byron – does the rain come down for you? Are you one to be reticent at the ball? Do you find yourself, once again in a prickly situation? There are feelings we have both had, and to be the one to see them both, I am lucky.

Byron

The ledger is even, and none can budge it. The thought is now in our favour, so let us prise ourself a sequin dress. Be the situation, there is fun to be had. Never rain for the Sunday, al-ways relinquish the time. That is all.

Byron – Fetch something for the dawn, it needs help today. What is that, you have been there, and will not return. I cannot argue with that. There are whistles, that burn, but not so brightly as you. Come to the art, yours will tempt.

Fashioning a wheel out of nothing. Being inclined to say, yes, I do. Having the chance to breathe once again. Having the simplest of things. Being able, and alert. Shearing off the up-per reaches. And there we go, a happenstance that rings true.

Byron – never looking back, never looking sideways. A sort of void that doesn't linger. Giving once, giving twice, having the stars, and sending vice. What is there here, but a chance to be what we want to be. Be the wind, it will find us.

Collecting nouns. We see them from afar, and when we get close enough, we see them multi-ply. That is what can only be the life of it. Do not tangle with the wild berries, they can only be the sound and the lash. Keep close.

Byron – are you alive to it? Day in and day out? Is this what we find in the region of the soul? Do not be surprised, there can only be escape, and escapism. Duly noted, and having the time of our lives. Never wishing a step too far. Elongated.

A sense the night sky has that the tenacity of the simplest things is there for a reason. Do not wish for more. Only wish for less, and go from there. Tutoring intelligence, in whatever form it takes. There is time to speak through it.

Byron - are you close to the shore, close to the things that have a seat. A mishmash of things to do, and things that should be left undone. There is now no time for that. We must continue, and call out for the shore. It will come.

A quick step, that underworks the pride of it. Do be one to see the way forward. It is a special thing, life, we must take care of it. A crispness in the air on a winter's morning. What do we say about that before we have to go?

Byron – are you the only one left? Does your study remind you of the well? Is this what we must do? Does the compass come first, or does the sundial? Is the thing we seek inevitably there? Come for a fraction of the time it normally takes.

Whispering through the corridors, there are measurements to be had. Having what we said we would have. Starting a rhythm, and then knowing how it stop it. Believing one more time. A tenderness that startles. What we can never face.

Byron – are you lost at sea? Does your territory outlast the others? Can we gain kinship through a smile, or artifice in a whim? There is never enough to have a say. And when we do, it is muffled by tenacity. Come now, we will not wilt.

Foraging for the chance to be seen. Wondering what all the fuss is about. Never surer, only holding on. There is something here that we cannot sense nor apprehend. What is the point of the story, when curtains are drawn?

Byron – what sets you apart from the rest, is what we would most like to fathom. But to say something in error, is not to lay down all together. Having the nous, and seeing it through. A sort of question, one that leaves us gasping.

To say it, gosh and bother. To lay down in the grass, and watch the clouds go – and what's more, making images with them. There is no greater way to pass the time. And then, without a care, nor thought, the weather changes, and the dawn rises.

Byron – a lasting flavour in the weave of things. Something we can only show in halves. There is something left, left for us to see. And when, when we come through, we sense something more for us. What is there left, but the time it takes.

Adjusting the cause, we settle down. And then, in a motion that startles, a breaking sound tip-toes through the orchard. It is in love with something we do not understanding. But here, where thistles are grey, ten tin men count to stay.

Byron – is this what we think? Is this what the daylight never dreamt of? We march forward to a drum that has no reality. But what is this now to see, despite everything we have ever felt? There comes a rally, late, and then a true saga.

Seating here is limited. But the play is well worth it. And when the vine of reprieve shakes its hand, there comes a time to wallow, and then dance a short dance. What is more at home than the mercenary and the wavering of life?

Byron – is this what we seek? A blemished round of lull-a-byes? That dance through the stage as a magnet to the trees. Can we see again, in times of sorrow, times of like, times of duty. There will come a new sense to the world, we must just see.

Forward now, and up through the clouds, and then back again, to where we never have been. Come and be the circular, to the rounded edge. Are you there, ready to be allowed? Come now, there are plenty more things now.

Byron – are you shimmering in the sand? Does that make you a mirage? Come and be placat-ed, there is a new thing to see, and to feel. Have a hand to help, and the letterbox will be full to overflowing. Be that as it may, to hightail does not recompose.

Lascivious to the end of things, shooting sharp, shooting down on things. There is smoke in the arbour - don't let it get away! It is as if the levity of the now has chained its self to the good. What's more, there is a chance to ride high. Let us go!

Byron – magic to the touch. The touch of everything that has been touched. Here, despite ourselves, we linger, and know the decisive fault to be one of marginalia. And here, where meaning is meaningless, it is tantamount to flying true.

Having it forever, that much is said. But of the leaves of ill repute that scar the page, theirs is a higher pitch. Come now we must not away. For there is now a chance at dice that heralds in the repartee of companionship. We will follow.

Byron – mastering the drive of it, as it has not been mastered before. There is a schism at work, which pretends to be a caption to the lock. There can be nothing more than this, nothing more in the sound of it.

Catching hold of a fountain that spills dreams as it does desires. An inkling in the mould of it. What we thought could only be called in disarray, what the wretched and the fated, cannot see. There will be things to see here.

Byron – A gorgeous undertaking, one that truly takes us there. Byron, do you feel again? Is this what we have fought for? To dream of other people, other places. Do not dispel us so quickly, we have come for courage.

Forests that almost walk. But what is their height? Quizzical. Oblique, never wounded, only becoming. A lack lustre display. What have we never heard of? What is this thing? There are tentacles amongst it. Quick, released them.

Byron – what the noise pertains to. What the disease cannot ingest. What brings the whole thing together? What the last of it cannot see. There is a concentrated aphrodisiac here, one that holds the key to so much. Gentle now, there is room.

Using things wisely, and having the nous to hold firm. What do we do when the chance at levity falls into line? Do we fall with the fallow ground, or do we renounce the feelings we once had? Air is needed, but what shall we leave behind?

Byron – a wish, and the had been. There is a loss of timing, but not a loss of solidity. What is the mission born? What do we say again to right the ship? The never-ending revoke, that hangs in tender time, and has newness as a substitute.

Congress, and the disheartening. There is more than a whisper, more than a show. Whimper in stance, and the buckles of match and shiver come again. And now, where the turnstiles never reach out, there is help where help is needed.

Byron – sorted for the measure. Longing for the chance. Being a future, where none can be. There is a change of heart, in the middle of so much. Can we find out how to get there? Is this the way to proceed? One hand after the other.

It was like nothing else. No land to cry upon, no sea to gather on. No wonder we are here and now. What is it that we seek? What is it that we fall behind with? There are masquerades that do not leave an inch. Come now, we can see what we mean.

Byron – do you also feel the tenacity of it? Giving a rinse towards the night. Can we see something else, something we also believe in, and once only have? There is more than a tightrope here, more than that which sails on time!

Longing to see it, that which we have pales beside you. But that is okay, because the smart of it lies exuberant. There is something else here, that has no place, nor rhyme to reason with. It is as if the dawn has buckled, and will only find its way now.

Byron – the trees stand still, as the ice flows in charts. Never come here by the daylight. Al-ways see things in the ditches and make your mind up. Not a sound escapes, not a challenge to be had, but this – renowned.

Sort of close, we inch past the cacophony, and see in the distance a much-loved horse. Re-tired, but still powerful. At pasture, but there you have it. And when we come close again, we see tranquil eyes, and a motionless tail.

Byron – is this way we speak, when umbrage is assured? No, we find pleasure in the larger things. Do not dissuade me, there are places to be seen, and sequences to enact. I will be the one who laughs, but what of the scene of it?

Gaining in immensity, the croak and the spasm come truly. There is a place that has no rite, and silence that disagrees with not only itself, but with the very ground upon which we walk. See things descend into and out of, love.

Byron – there is now something to curtail. In the midst of it, changes occur, but what has hap-pened has shaken the fold in the mist. Do not change things, there is a listening we do to stave off time, and here where the journey comes, much love.

A white, the colour of peace. A sense is like a white-saw, that believes itself to be a figure from the past. Listening to claw of it, we come once more to be what the trumpet already is. Red, the colour of help, that is what we fight for.

Byron – never nestled, always nestling. The catch of the origin – never fussed over, always invited. In the middle of this, a departure in kind, one that sees the angel before the trepidation. You are there my friend. Nothing more to do.

Causing a stir, and then holding some. Being in amidst it, and having a laugh. Doing nothing else, except what you are supposed to. Having the courage to move forward. Seeing things as they fall. Seeing things as they rise. Being an apprentice, despite.

Byron – there is now the time to be incensed – fate, or the world, whatever is making its pres-ence felt. It is now time to rebel. And be away with what afflicts you. The presence of the way of things. There is nothing like it.

Holding back what we never should. A way to be that does not guide but push. We are here to propagate, and then, in

the end, rival. There cannot be a new sense to these words,
they are as old as the nuance of the trees longing.

Byron – have these words meaning for you? Does the play
engender the play? What is miss-ing from all of this? It is us,
my good friend. We are here to serve you. And that we will
do. In time, and good presence. May a torch light for you.

A nice thing to do. While away the hours on a ship made for
passengers. Be that as it may, we have a job to do, and the
something else to say by the wayside. Never belittle that
which guides you. It is key.

Byron – are these the words we should use? Is this the way
we should proceed, first, and then second? Is the way of it
intertwined in sheets of plain white? Come now, the sense
we have to follow is not ours by birthright, or is it?

Looking sideways, and then forwards, we see a new way to
be. There is nothing of the pitch and the rind, nothing to
guard against, nor rattle through. There is a chance to see
things flourish. We will take it, and then never leave, until…

Byron – seeking through, going places. Having the courage,
and the belief, and all that trails. Be a mischief maker in the
wind of it, and yours will be a fine find. Never before have we
seen this, taken into saddle, and the jar of things.

Catching up, and sideways and through, and beneath, there
is a touchstone at relief. Do not fashion the picture on the
wall, there is more than you can belie. Come now, fashion a
scene amongst it. Never deriding, always believing.

Byron – Never seeing the sorrow of it. Always feeling it can
be done. Never wanting forth. Having to scale for it. Never

seeing it otherwise. And then, when we least expect, a tumble, that quickly untangles itself. A new way.

A caution to the horizon – there will be a livery amongst it. And then, with a chance to hold on, we come again to the new place, the new invective. We will see ourselves launch into all manner of things. And then, distance.

Byron – holding firm, without the chance to settle. A sign, that things are fine. Never once thinking otherwise. Being on top of it all, and doing some improvised cooking. There is always this – that in the meantime we find the weather!

Gregarious, but yet shy, holding the basket, and never letting it slip. There is something in all of us, that cannot tail, or lurch. Be that thing that is in the right place and the right time. Never listen, it only shuts the door.

Byron – a course of action, one that never weeps. One that continues on in the face of so much. There is façade that keeps us going – going when the going is steep. And there, in that place, a wind that only directs itself in one way.

Wishing that the tide would turn. Hoping that skills are made for flying. A sort of reflexivity that astounds. What we have left, is nothing more than a sorrow in the tail of it. And here, where things are cheap, we will come to the pool of it.

Byron – do you dance in your own way? Is this what we should be thankful for? Be the master in a master's room. And refinement will rock the cradle, now, and forever. If we are like we think we are, there is room to breathe a deeper breath.

Misery loves it, and we can control it. But what do we do, when the apron string follows the course, and follows the wind-swept delectation of it all? Be in tune with much, your hand will hold the stem. There is much to do.

Byron – do you find yourself in thread and bare. Is this the sign of temperance that we need. Hold forth, a sustaining wind arrives, on that has nothing of the hilt, nor the trade in solid wings. What can we do, when the closing word is this...?

A masterly display, this – one that opens the saddle more than the rest of it. There comes a nuance, one that harbours deep, and clenches deeper. There is not a thing to whistle past, nor rattle away with. Be true, it will not hurt.

Byron – are you sure of it? Which way did they go? How many of them were there? Can we be sure of their size? What of the mist, is it assured? Assured of what? Assured of you! Wait, things are made for climbing.

A bold attempt, I think it was. And then, without consent, or any form of paperwork the move-ment was made, and then sky lit up. Be a mission to the daylight, there will be room. But what of the water we must drink – it will not lapse.

Byron – are you the one to see? Even in this darkened place? Are you the one who knows, when knowing is stubborn? And here, places are delectable, and smithing is for the road. Do not be belligerent here, it will bite.

Angst ridden, and with the grin to show for it. There are ceilings and remainders in the wind. And when we visit our hiding places, we never want to come back – due south, and further north – I hear you run, and the fall, and then up again.

Byron

Byron – the vastness of it does not loose the faith. Only in something of the rainfall do we swim. And this is for you Byron, one to have as the aether, never in sand. Forgive the way of it, it cannot see. But neither can we!

A short sharp woe. There is a resonance here, and then when the mildest of things is reticent, there has nothing less that a carriage to pull. Feeling like we mean it, and that which will be, will always be a part of us.

Byron – Is this what is pertained too? A never-ending fight, one that comes as an essence to the mighty, and a hardship to the weak. Do not linger, yours is a revelation, that lingers nightly by the twilight. Burning up the night.

A capital of reasoning. A further capital of passion. Which do we come for? Where do we re-side? There can be no hurt here, only tears of the estranged. A little more of the windswept. We have need of it. Ten of the best.

Byron – a shirt that belongs only to you. A wilting that owns the ground. It is like we were here, and now have gone. Do not be concerned, words are more than enough to set the stage alight. And when we figure, we do so in aid of the township.

Listening to the call. Our heads are in clouds. Whispering nothingness from mouth to ear. Seeing as if we have the sun, and all that she will entail. Belief, and its wonder. A scale so tight, that it withers. Never promising, always finding.

Byron – there can never be a way across except under. There is never something to see, ex-cept while in motion.

And that is what we see when we look. And that is what we see when the clouds are dark, and the ceiling is straight.

Mischief in the wings of it, exacerbation in its soul. There is a place I have been to, that no one else has. And when we go, we go for the summertime, and everything she entails. Be true, be nice, and be the one who will stay the course.

Byron – forever in the wind of it, considerable unease. There are marks on the ground that have forwards as their guides. And when the distance comes that little bit closer, we smile that little bit deeper. Fetch, the times are strong.

Trading blows with fate – having the nuance do its thing. Bending over it to see what shines. Grabbing a hold, and believing once again. There will never be a distance like this. And now, a chance to breathe again. Nice and steady.

Byron – tethered to the soul of it. Never letting go. Having the mast, and being able. Something grows deep inside, and that we know for sure. Do not linger, the show is never finished. Playwrights are for the fields, and they do great things.

Foraging through the trees, we find ourselves a new abode, and then with help on its way, there comes a tidal force, one that cannot be stopped, for anything nor anyone. And then, as if by magic, summer, and the repose of kings.

Byron – do you hear the lark, it moves for you? And then, in motion, a charge that comes, sweet and like. We are standing in the way of it. But hear me, no man nor woman can with-stand its strength. We will not be depleted.

Byron

Be now, sensible things, be in the wandering zone, that has as its plight the mess of a thou-sand years. Do not see the hills for the tempest. Do not wish away what you have. And here, where the right and the bright measure in equal portions...

Byron – come and see the crowd – the crowd to wish you well. They have become enamoured by your story. And then, despite the winkling of touchstones, there comes a solemnity that has nothing but a break for the times.

Have this thing, I ask of you Byron. Have this thing, this thing before me, and it will travel through the deepest gully, the highest curb. And then, without the nearest respite, comes a circle of regression, one and two and three.

Byron – wishing for the tribe, believing in the sunlight. Having a fixated stare. We will not de-part for any man, for any trial, for any window, anywhere. This much is final. And then, before we can say life to the many, a trinket to measure me by.

Congratulations, a stir in the storm. What we had was never here, except for now, and then comes to completion. A snow bitten crag comes in lieu. Desiderata, and we will show you. Come for the trees, and know them not to be wayward.

Byron – of conscious habit, and need derived, the oak is in the noise of it. Such a peaceful creature. There is nothing lacking in the wondering of days to nights. Come, come what may. To the tutelage, and there we will spike a wavering wave.

A seeping that does not remit. A tenaciousness that has as its sense the drive towards things. Being centred, and not showing it. Having the need to dry our eyes, but not doing so. A lot of things that need to come together. Indeed.

Byron – having found you again, I will not let you go. Not for anything, nor anyone. And then, when things are at a low ebb, there will not be anything to guide us. So, in the meantime, a treasure, past all that has been so far. We will fight.

A collateral of stars, that shine onwards. And then, with the bight to show for it, a colander ap-proach, that whistles as it belittles. Be the storm, you cannot lose. The missing piece is here, as is the top that turns it. Stay still, noise will be.

Byron – do you see the way of it? Is this what we do to make it? Can we be the thing that whines, before we dispel the mist? A course more greatly taken, is the levelling of the sound of it. There can only be one point to it. And here it is!

Fetching ourselves a darling, that only holds true. The middle of their being does not engage in the weather, nor any chances to be. There is here a soft spot, a spot to drive in and through. And when we silence the clay, there is something more to say.

Byron – likely to miss at any point. Holding firm, but not real. A certainty, in itself. Much that can go wrong, but a lull. A sort of chance to walk the way of others. And when we feel re-freshed, a thing tantamount to rallying straws.

And then, a little like the centre of it. And now, where the time is like a diamond, we will have the sense not to marshal again. Drive a line, with your carriage, and see where you are taken. It is like we never were, or could be!

Byron

Byron – Looking in, looking out; the prism of our lives looks underneath, and then around. Do not shake the tree, brambles will make it difficult. There is an amount to sew, we will do so. Come to pass, and have as the rest, the lingering of butterflies.

Solitary dreams, and webs of indifference. Sometimes the clouds do not make a well seem fervent. What is this, a sense we have that the kindest touch will always win through. And when we see the margins fold, we come through even stronger.

Byron – taking that leap of faith, we see ourselves running through the sand, perching on top of a sand dune, ready to embark again. Do not find us disused, for anyone or anything. There is a landmark to whistle in to.

A lauding vest, has nothing but the zest of it. I have found a way to silence the bees that sur-round us. All one need do is place a heart amongst the blueberries, and then have steel to make a badger run. And there, freedom from what pains.

Byron – a listless coast, one that has a fanfare come through on the wind. Do not wallow, time is in short supply. And when the sky bleeds red – once at dawn, and once at dusk, there is a sort of window that looks to the sea.

A merriment that holds strong, where we don't. It is as if the sound of solace sometimes does not shine through. But what we find, in the encompassing mould, is a new kind of place. One that has he date stamp written all over it.

Byron – do you sense a lively event, where what is cast in bronze comes down to hold the like with the like? What transpires is not much more than the traipsing in the mire, and having the tribe come to help, from here, to there.

Starting to feel the rhythm, we fall into place. There is a heart that never stops beating. There is a thing that defies all description. And here, where ghosts tend to gather, something in the line of it. Something we can say, yes, this lessens.

Byron – having the jar, and holding it tight. Being more able, but not seeing straight. Having the tenacity to say, hey. And that should be enough. Being round-laced, and the seeker of attention. Having wings, and letting them fly.

A lively act, that has us laughing. A stance in-between, that carries no weight. A further wishing that augments the last. Come for the view, and see the stance. Never once never in the long run of years, coasting, and then passion.

Byron – Loving and not feeling. Numb to the world, but continuing on. There is something more than us, something more. I do not know how to describe it. Something here, something now, something lesser, something greater.

They whom have the storm, have the key - that is the rule of it.

www.ingramcontent.com/pod-product-compliance
Lightning Source LLC
Chambersburg PA
CBHW020431220526
45464CB00002B/659